AHUAPAN COMBAT ESKRIMA

AHUAPAN COMBAT ESKRIMA

Filipino Martial Art

Volume 1

GREG SILHOL

THOMAS ROUSSEL

Toucher le sol, en général on s'en remet
On en renaît pas toujours plus fort, mais on fait l'effort
Faut maintenir la soif, celle du lendemain
Y'a pas de mais, à nouveau se relever sinon c'est mort

Combien de fois on s'est dit, ça y est ce coup-là c'est fini ?
Ces jours où il y avait plus de force ou plus d'envie
Mais je crois que c'est écrit dans nos gènes, comme respirer
On se remettra toujours en selle, prêts à transpirer

IAM, "Bien plus Beau"

To Léa and Anthony

This book is also in memory of our brother in arms Laurent Gutierrez…

Table of Contents

Foreword

As countless other martial artists, and numerous other teenagers of the eighties, I grew up at a time deeply marked by the figure of Bruce Lee, actor with an athletic style and a yell as identifiable as the one of Tarzan (another emblematic figure of the moment). Strangely, I discovered my first movie of Bruce Lee rather late... It was 'Return of the Dragon', if I remember correctly. Until then, a few extracts, a famous poster and the imitations of a few friends trying to manipulate with agility a nunchaku were enough to construct his legend for me...

Fascinated by the image of martial arts, I couldn't bring myself to start any (and one comes up with all kinds of excuses for that...). A Judo free trial class in a municipal activity center in Marseille, then a few months of Shotokan Karate at the university of Montpellier, were my only two incursions in that domain before I was thirty years old. I then thought of myself as a lost cause for the world of Martial Arts (not that it would care much...). But it turned out otherwise thanks to the perseverance of my entourage (as it happens, my wife and my friend Anthony), who made up a real conspiracy to register me in a club — a minimum to defeat my 'I'm getting too old for this shit' attitude.

Here I was, black pants and white T-shirt on, for my first class of Wing Tsun Kung Fu, Leung Ting system... again in the shadow of Bruce Lee, who in his time had learn the Wing Chun in Hong Kong, in the school of the now famous grandmaster Ip Man. My new professor was not unknown to me as we had met and sympathized in another context. He is still today the sifu who leads my progression and discovery of that Chinese martial art: Sifu Fabrice, chief instructor of the Wing Shun schools in France. I was now in the footsteps of the 'Little Dragon', and somehow much more than I thought.

We can debate over the real martial aptitudes of Bruce Lee. Was he, after all, only a 'good' actor of action movies? Well, I never met him, I never exchanged a few punches with him... but I think he was both, a martial artist and movie artist, in order to stand out even nowadays, and maintain his legend and his influence in martial arts several decades after his death. He was a genius, a visionary, who had integrated the Filipino Martial Arts to the teachings of his own style, the Jeet Kune Do, as a result of his friendship and work with one of his students, Dan Inosanto. And we could find that influence in the European Wing Tsun schools which offered, 'quite naturally', the teaching of the Latosa Escrima, style developed by Rene Latosa, who had been a student of Angel Cabales, founder of the Serrada Escrima.

It was not one martial art I was starting for my thirties, but two. On one side a Kung Fu style based on the human (by comparison with other styles with animal references), fast, efficient, which learning process starts with a feet/fists work, and then weapons only in its advanced form. On the other side, the art of the warriors of the Southeast Asian archipelago, where one starts with the weapons to take up only later the bare hands techniques. Two different arts, which meet in many principles, as the center line, the muscular relaxation, the triangle, the flow of the techniques done one after another… 'Be water my friend'…

I owe to internet my encounter with Guro Thomas Roussel. From one discussion group to another, led by curiosity, I had acquired a good idea of the interesting professors and of the other styles taught in France. His name came back several times. But I did not expect to enter in contact with him so quickly. I even didn't know I was as he answered my post over the thermoplastic eskrima sticks made by the famous knife brand Cold Steel. Only when he invited me to Lyon for a seminar in his school did I realized he was that Thomas Roussel, one of the few experts of Kali Eskrima in France, and the only one who had won three European titles, and one World title in the United Kingdom, in its competitive form. I met and sympathized afterward with some other members of that circle of the French experts of the FMA, as Fabien Jolivel, Stéphane Pourre or Michel Rozzi. But I must acknowledge that my encounter with Thomas stays as one that stands out in a life, as it was the case earlier when I met Fabrice. I feel lucky for all the happy and enlightening friendships that I have built, and am still building, in the course of my practice (and they are numerous). But I'm even luckier to have found on my way not only one, but two professors and friends.

From that 'competitive combat' seminar in Lyon, my first experiment with the 'competitive ' aspect of the Kali Eskrima, I came out covered with bruises, delighted and won over by the teaching method, the generosity and the efficiency of Guro Thomas. A few months later, a second encounter on a sunny square of Montpellier followed by a meal at my home which stretched in discussions until dawn, and our friendship and collaboration were born. I then became a student of the Ahuapan Combat Eskrima group. And as I could not follow the class of the gym at 'Sword Street' ('rue de l'Epée', that is truly the name of the street) in Lyon, I organized seminars with Guro Thomas Roussel in Montpellier as often as possible. On the solid foundations that my learning of the Latosa Escrima had built, I discovered, with the Ahuapan group, the variety and the subtlety of the Filipino Martial Arts, developing further my flow and enhancing me with Doble Baston, disarms, knife, Panantukan or Espada y Daga… And each seminar, each master class or private lesson, was an occasion to write page after page in my notebooks.

It is the result of these notebooks, and my thoughts over the teachings and the transmission of the style developed by Punong Guro Thomas Roussel, that I offer you to discover in this book — or at least a first part as two or three volumes may be necessary to present an overview of these teachings. Books and films will never replace the direct teaching of a professor, or practice itself. But they can be solid 'aide-mémoire' or vectors of discovery. This is my only claim here, to participate in the share of the FMA, through the style I know the best, and provide to the students and instructors a book to refer to.

Mabuhay, live well…

Guro Greg Silhol, Montpellier 2017.

Ahuapan Combat Eskrima

The practice of Martial Arts, whatever their geographic origins, is in essence a progression, personal and individual in some respects, but not solitary...

Some practitioners will walk briskly, others will take their time, taking sometimes a break or some back roads... What is important from my point of view is to carry out that journey in full consciousness, in order to take advantage of the landscape and improve from the experiences lived on the way...

And all the way, we are led to meet people... some to guide us, indicate us the direction to take or the one to avoid, others to 'walk' with us for a time... This book, that you are about to discover, is precisely the fruit of one of these meeting — I won't tell you again about the circumstances, that Greg has already explained — and of the shared experiences while travelling together.

I had the chance, in the past, to do myself some inspiring encounters while going on the martial way, for more than three decades now. Among them, some have directed me on ways I had no idea they existed, others have been, or are still, fellow travellers... and the hardness of the progress has allowed us to forge friendships of an unfailing solidity.

My first guide on that road of life was a Karate sensei, Georges Vallecchia, with whom I have learned to move. I have also begun to foresee the potential personal development that could be achieved through the training in a martial discipline. And above all, as he was quite open-minded — I underline this here as it was not the norm in the Karate milieu of the eighties in the area of Nice — I had the chance to meet another sensei. He taught disciplines I didn't knew about, other than one was the style of Bruce Lee, the Jeet Kune Do. The other was the Kali Eskrima. Didier Trinocque was one of the first French who had the opportunity to study these fighting arts.

I must admit that from the very start the Jeet Kune Do literally subjugated me with the richness of possibilities that the art offered in comparison with what I knew, the Karate. The Kali Eskrima on the other hand seemed to me a very technical discipline, not enough brawling oriented in the eyes of the teenager eager of strong sensations that I was then.

My meeting with Sifu/Guro Didier Trinocque has certainly been an important step in my development as a martial artist, technically but also in my way of thinking about my practice. These reflections led me some years later to reconsider my point of view about the Filipino fighting arts and, as he had done himself, to leave and seek answers abroad, as he had left the area of Nice and even France at that time.

So, a chance reading led me to get in touch with another guide whose impact on my progress in the understanding of the fighting arts, and notably those which originate from the Filipino archipelago, was the more decisive... Tuhon Patrick O'Malley, British expert, colorful, genuine and rustic, to whom I owe a very large part of my understanding of the road covered.

I had the privilege to study under his supervision for more than ten years, several months a year, following the method known in the Japanese traditions under the term uchi-deshi (resident student), enriching experience to the highest level.

Some years ago, almost ten, took place the first great multi-styles seminar of Filipino Martial Arts organized in France — an event where I was invited as a contributor and on the occasion of which the organizers (Stéphane Fernandez and Sigfried Lepeu) asked me to give a name to the school I was to represent...

I had taken some distance with the organization I was with at that time, I so 'created' a name to designate my school. But, not in the idea that I thought I had created a new style — I had not and I still don't have that claim — but rather in the idea by which groups are forming in the Brazilian fighting art of Capoeira. There is two major styles but plenty of groups...

And so I formulated *Ahuapan* — not a Tagalog or Cebuano term as you may think but Panoan, a local language of Peru, that means "of the tapir", with reference to an alias that I used in some internet forums dedicated to martial arts — *Combat* — as I am firmly convinced of the virtues and learnings gained from the regular exercise of combat — *Eskrima* — of course with reference to the generic term that designate the armed Filipino Martial Art, synonym itself of the terms Arnis or Kali.

I chose to teach Eskrima some fifteen years ago, and I have the luck to have created a small circle of motivated and assiduous students, that have been with me for more than ten years and are now my assistants. Some of them have chosen to use the competitive form of our discipline as a vehicle on the Way, in which they made me proud with several titles won.

Among that small circle, there is one particular student as he does not live near the place where I give my classes and most of my seminars. But he is nonetheless motivated and assiduous, and he have achieved progress as an eskrimador, that I can see at each of our meeting, but also as an instructor. That again I can see realizing the evolution of his own students when I come in his school to direct a seminar...

That student — you have easily guessed I was talking about the author of the present book, Greg — does me today the great honor to make a work of presentation of our school, of our group (of which he is a full member). This book, I hope, will be an inspiration to the readers who want to feed their thought about that exotic art stemmed from the traditions of the jungles of the Southeast Asian archipelago, but nevertheless remarkably contemporary by the pragmatism of its tactical material.

A book does certainly not replace the benefits of learning with a competent instructor. And, even if our disciplines are still rather confidential in France, there is a number of strongly experimented instructors, from different styles, who offers classes and seminars throughout our country... But a book of quality may be a first step, a meeting in a kind of way, that will guide and direct the practitioner on the Way... a direction that he may choose to follow for a short or a long time.

I end these few lines by addressing my thanks to all the 'sensei' I had the honor and the privilege to meet on my way, and whom took some times to share with me their experiences, thoughts and learnings in order to help me going each time a step farther. The list is long and I cannot name all of them. But I will address particularly my gratitude to my mentor since I'm in the Lyon area, Franky Clifford Ledée, as to my brothers in arms Eric Cervel, Sylvio Silveri and the youngest Jean-Yves Castellano...

Punong Guro Thomas Roussel, Lyon 2017.

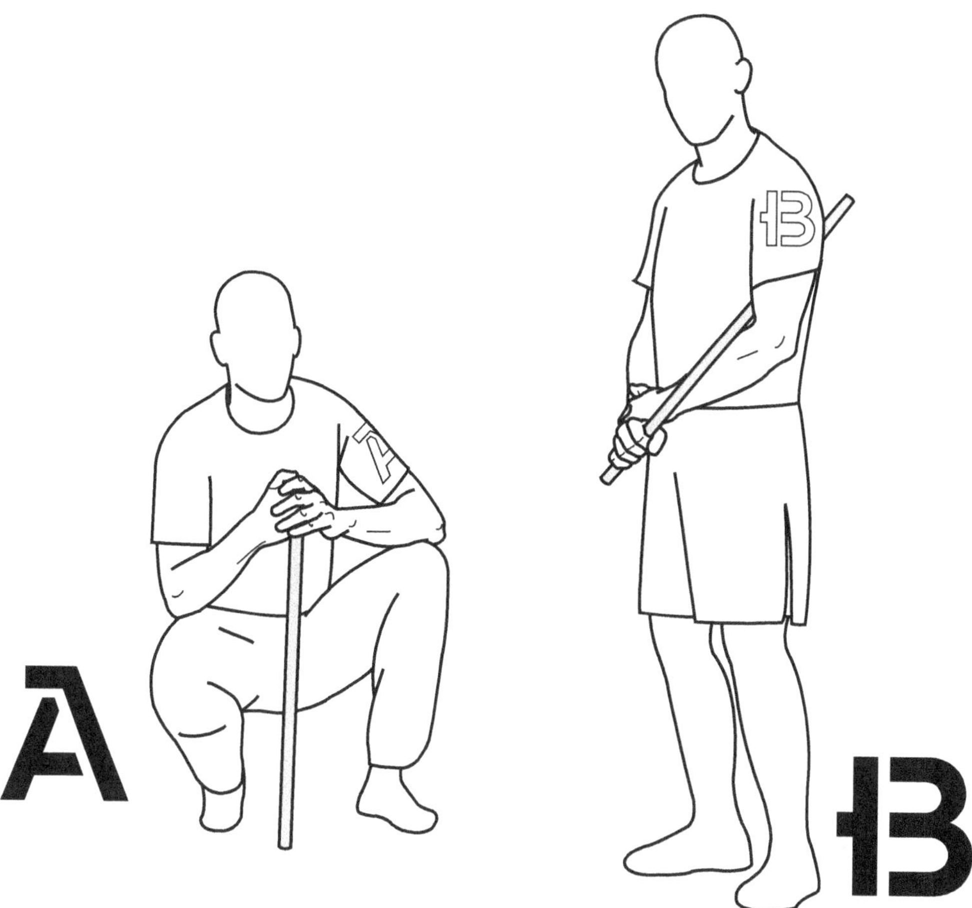

A and B, students of the Ahuapan Combat Eskrima group, will guide us all the way through this book and will display the exercises.

Grips, Stance, Guards
and Angles

I. GRIPS

As a martial art, the learning process of Eskrima focuses first on the practice of weapons. Its bare hands variations — percussions, grabs, locks,… — ensue from the principles, body mechanics and angles acquired with the work of the weapons, or more simply are considered as advanced work.

The favored tool to get familiar with the practice of the weapons is the stick (olisi in Tagalog,…). Its length and diameter can vary from one style of Eskrima to another, from one practitioner to another. In Ahuapan we will generally prefer a stick about 28 inches (70 cm) in length and 1 inch (2,5 cm) in diameter.

PAIR OF RATTAN STICKS, METAL TRAINING KNIFE, HOCKEY GLOVES, HELMET WITH FACEMASK…

The important thing to understand and keep in mind, is that Eskrima is not a Martial Art of the stick. Eskrima is a Martial Art of armed combat. If the stick is indeed a weapon, it is fundamental to consider it here as a tool with which we can train our body and our fighting skills to use a great array of weapons.

So, even with a stick in hand, the practitioner of Eskrima must 'imagine' the position of the edge of the blade (and we agree that there is no edge on a stick), in order to train for correct strikes. This is achieved by directing the line formed by the central joints of the fingers towards the target...

To hit without considering that warning would be, once armed with an edged weapon, like striking with the flat of the blade. Moreover, even with a blunt weapon, we would then risk to disarm ourselves, the hand being orientated in the opening direction of the fingers.

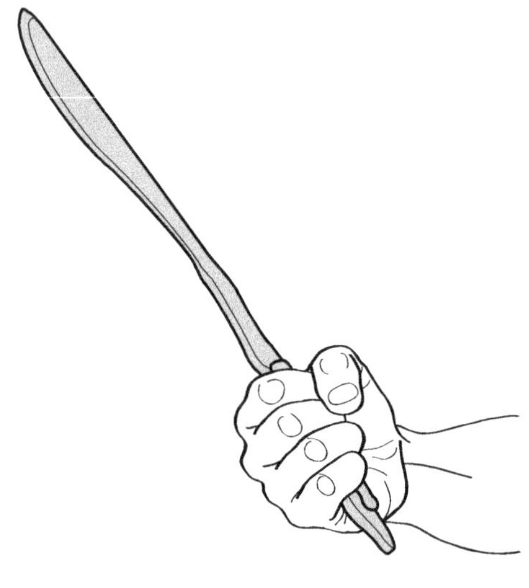

The grip on the stick is done with full hand, neither too tight, nor too loose — the idea of the little bird in our hand that we must not let either suffocate or evade is relevant here. It is a grip called Hammer Grip. During manipulations, we will be careful not to open the fingers, as although it may give a wrong impression of ease, the chances of being disarmed at the impact increase greatly.

The stick is held by an end, keeping one to three fingers length of stick free between the end of the stick and the hand. That part is called the *Punyo*. Its first utility is that we do not lose our stick immediately when it gets slippery. We can also use the punyo to hit at short range, disarm or control, as it will be described in the following chapters.

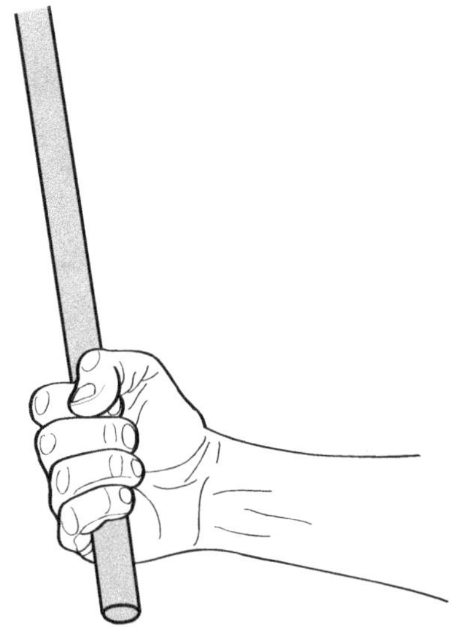

It is not quite relevant to grab our stick by the middle (although it may be seen in some warm up exercises for the wrist). However, in the work of Dos Manos, we grab our stick with our two hands, respectively placed at each end.

With long blades, the grip is very similar to the one of the stick — we may however adapt to the specificity of a particular blade and its handle.

Shorter objects like knives, but also pens, flashlights,... can be held in two different grips. The 'Hammer' grip, the same as for the stick, and the 'Ice Pick' grip.

For a standard knife (these considerations may vary for some specific types of knives):

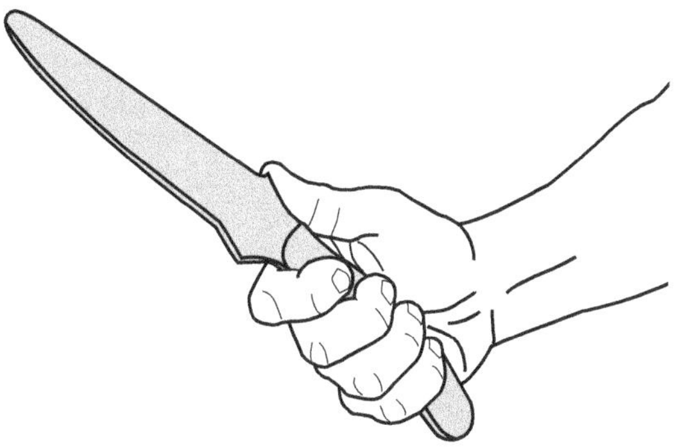

— in the Hammer grip, the thumb, that covers the forefinger and the middle finger when holding the stick, is here better placed in line with the back of the blade. In this way it prevents the hand to slip on the edge, but also it helps to manage the penetration in the target.

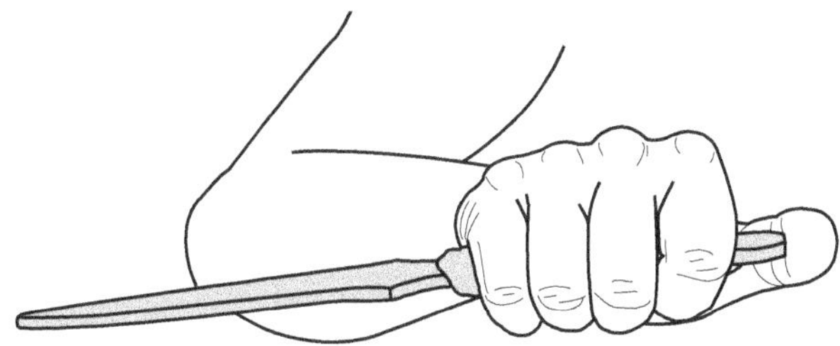

— in the Ice Pick grip it is important to hold the knife with the edge on the opposite side from the forearm (directed towards the opponent and not towards us). The thumb is ideally placed on the end of the weapon. It increases the penetrating capacity and prevents the hand to slip on the edge.

II. STANCE

The fighting stance of the eskrimador, the practitioner of Eskrima, is rather natural. It is quite similar to the one of a modern boxer, except that the armed hand and the related foot are forward (a right-handed boxer will prefer to be in a left guard).

The legs are spread but not wider than the shoulder width. The weight of the body is supported by the front leg, in order to gain full advantage of the length of the weapon. If the front foot is flat on the floor, the heel of the back foot is detached from the floor, ready to thrust forward, as at the start of a race.

The torso is straight, full-face. The head is straight, the gaze wide. The alignment from the top of the head to the coccyx is kept, passing by the spinal column. We avoid to lean forward (and backward), to keep the balance.

The hands are raised on guard, elbows close to the body. Usually, the armed hand is held in front of the unarmed hand.

The shoulders are relaxed, and more generally, the whole body must be alert but relaxed. Tightness, and even more contraction must be proscribed. Relaxation allows to be reactive, explosive and adaptable, which is essential in combat. It also allows, despite common belief, to deliver powerful strikes, notably by the interaction of several parts of the body in the action. On the contrary, muscular contraction would act as a brake to the movement.

A right stance ensures balance, stability and power.

Needless to say that the stance described here will vary with movements, dodges and sidesteps. Nothing is frozen. Mobility is also essential, it is the key of the combat and so of the martial art.

III. GUARDS

The guard is both a passive defense and the initial stance from which active defenses and attacks are launched.

To be off-guard, is to lower its defenses and be compelled to do an unnecessary motion to launch an attack. One must be very confident to deliberately lower his guard.

Two main guards are distinguished here.

ABIERTA, THE 'OPEN' GUARD

The weapon is held in order for the point to aim at the opponent (and not only at the sky). The armed hand is behind the weapon (not at the same level). The unarmed hand is behind. When the two hands hold a weapon, the hand holding the longest is forward, the shortest behind — as in Espada y Daga (sword and dagger) work. The elbows are close to the body.

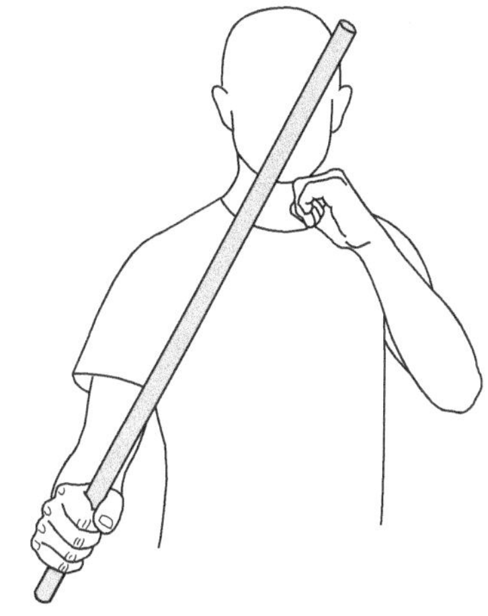

In some styles, it is recommended to stick the unarmed hand on the torso. In my humble opinion, it is better to keep it alert, at the level of the throat. So, the hand covers the neck, the forearm covers the heart, the elbow protects the ribs and the spleen, while still immediately available. In the following chapters, the great usefulness of that hand, although unarmed, will be demonstrated.

The abierta guard is, at middle range with a stick, a rather 'defensive' guard as it is not the best to initiate an immediate attack, unless a complementary motion is done. It is more 'offensive' with a blade or with a stick at long range (where the attack motion is developed during the stepping to close the distance). With a blade, the tip is pointed as a threat at the opponent. We can initiate an immediate thrust attack.

SERRADA, THE CLOSED GUARD

The weapon is held with the punyo towards the opponent, tip towards the back. The stick is on the left side.

The position of the unarmed hand is similar to the one in abierta guard.

It is a guard more appropriate for the stick, more 'offensive', from where several attacks in different angles can be initiate without any complementary motion.

Other guards do exist, and some variations of these two, such as the 'hidden' guards, relevant to conceal a short weapon before the first blow is delivered.

IV. NINE BASIC ANGLES, TWO TYPES OF STRIKES, FOUR TECHNIQUES...

An element shared by the different styles of Eskrima, as they are taught, is to reason in terms of angles for the attacks. And to tell the difference between the angles, a specific number is given to each angle — a same angle, however, may have a different number assigned from a school to another. What is important is the concept, the idea of a vector of attack, independent from the weapon used.

For example, whether it is launched with a stick, a machete, a pen or a knife, a forehand diagonal attack, from top to bottom, is a number 1 angle (by convention). So if the weapon is held with the right hand, it is an attack from right to left going downward. Caution! A blow given with the left hand, going downward from left to right (forehand) is also a number 1 angle!

If you are familiar with the concept of 'vector', it is easy to understand that the angle is independent from the height from which it has been performed. Even if, by convention, a preferential target is designated for each angle. So, if the side of the abdomen is generally the target of a number 3 angle, an horizontal forehand strike to the knee or the neck... is still a number 3 angle.

While teaching and in all the exercises described in this book, we will use the angles depicted by the following drawings to identify the strikes delivered (and the matching defenses).

NINE BASICS ANGLES

ANGLE 1

Forehand strike, in a downward diagonal. With a stick the target is generally the side of the head. With a blade, it is the neck.

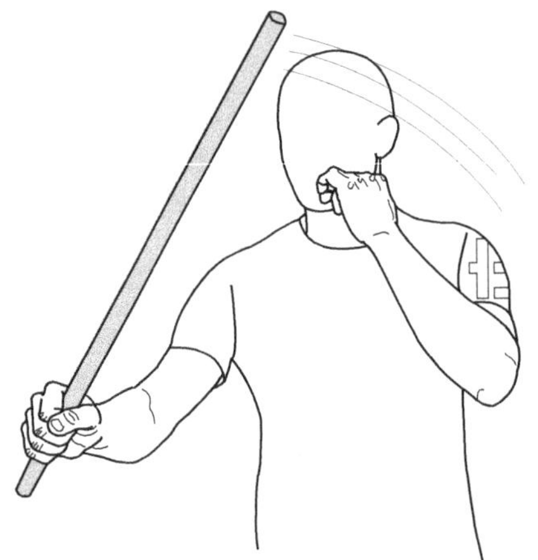

ANGLE 2

Backhand strike, in a downward diagonal. Same target as in the Angle 1.

ANGLE 3

Forehand strike, horizontal. The target is generally the side of the abdomen.

ANGLE 4

Backhand strike, horizontal. Same target as for the Angle 3.

ANGLE 5

Direct thrust slightly upward to the abdomen.

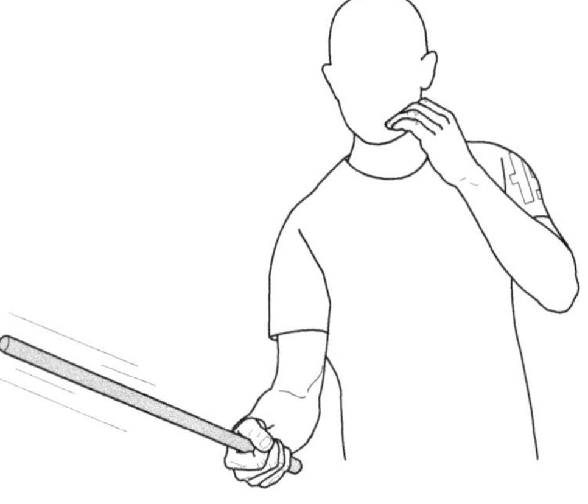

ANGLE 6

Backhand strike, in an upward diagonal. The target is generally the knee or the waist.

ANGLE 7

Forehand strike, in an upward diagonal. Same target as for the Angle 6.

ANGLE 8

Backhand thrust to the eye or the chest.

ANGLE 9

Forehand thrust to the eye or the chest.

TWO TYPES OF STRIKES

LOBTIK, GOING THROUGH STRIKES

The attack is delivered with the idea of going through the target. In an angle 1, the motion begins in the top right-hand corner and ends in the bottom left-hand corner.

The Lobtik is a fierce strike.

WITIK, SNAPPING STRIKES

The strike is delivered in order to snap on the target. The Witik is a blunt strike crisper and lighter than the Lobtik.

FOUR SPECIFIC TECHNIQUES

ABANIKO

Abaniko, a word borrowed to the Spanish language, means fan. This technique is referring to the surprising strikes delivered with a quick rotation of the wrist and the forearm (as to snap a fan open). The Abaniko can be done on an horizontal axis or on a vertical axis.

REDONDO

Backhand strike where the eskrimador makes a large circle on the vertical axis with his weapon. It is notably a formidable attack to strike the hand of the opponent while keeping away. The redondo is one of the circular strikes grouped together under the heading Kurbada.

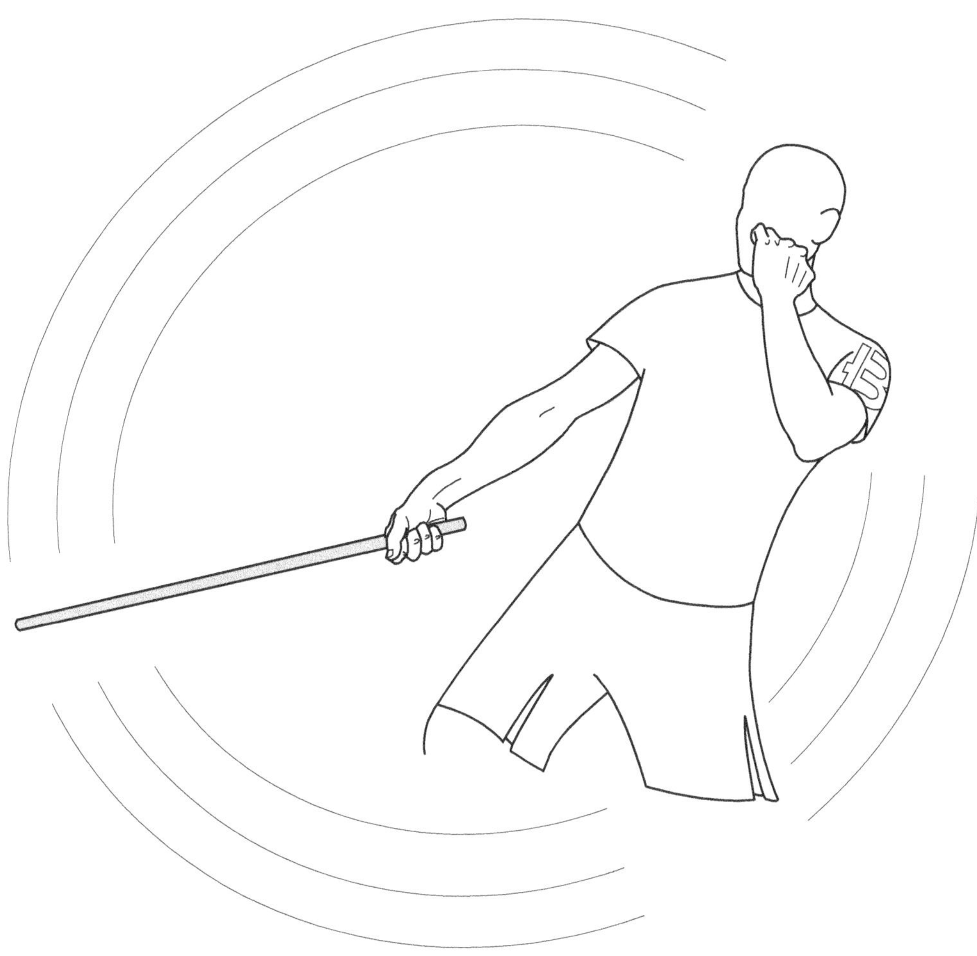

KURBADA

The eskrimador circles with his weapon. The circle can be large or small, on the vertical or the horizontal axis, forehand or backhand. It is an efficient technique with a blunt weapon or with a blade.

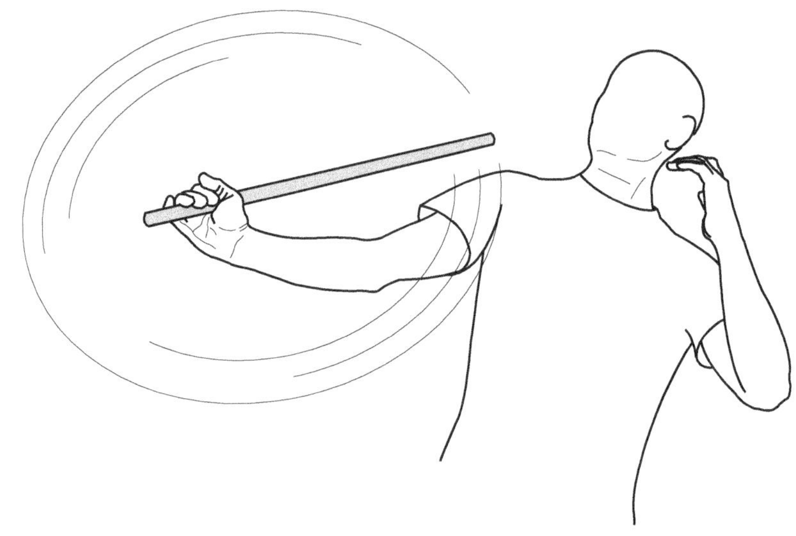

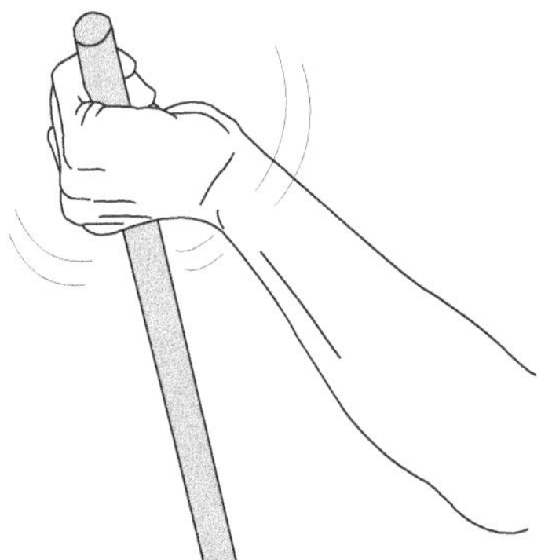

ARKO

The eskrimador rotates his wrist, forward or backward. The arko is used to warm up the wrist, and enhance the mobility of this joint. But in combat, the Arko is also useful to change the attack angle in the course of a motion or to strike again at short range, without moving the arm backward.

In order to describe the techniques and exercises of this book, we will use the following convention:

Angle 1 lobtik [R] , means 'forehand strike, downward diagonal, going through, the weapon being held in the right hand'.

Combat Ranges
& Footworks

I. COMBAT RANGES

In order to be at combat range, we must be able to touch a target on the adversary. If by stretching the arm and the weapon, we do not touch any constituent part of the opponent… we are off range. And then it will be necessary to move forward, or that the opponent moves forward, to be at range.

There are three combat ranges, that cannot be spelled in standard measure units, as they depend on the corpulences of the two adversaries facing each other, and the weapons they hold respectively. So a small man holding a stick may be at 'Long' range while his taller adversary holding a little knife is still 'off range'.

LARGO MANO, LONG RANGE

At that range it is still not possible to touch the trunk of the opponent with the weapon, but we can reach the hand.

It is a relevant range for the work with a long blade. It is also a range that should be prioritized when working with the double sticks (Doble Baston).

It allows to deploy powerful strikes, as a result of their amplitude and their inertia. They are difficult to block, but these attacks are more readable.

While training, to check that they do stand at Largo Mano range, the two partners are facing each other in fighting stance, arm stretched, stick stretched. The last 4 inches of the stick must be at the level of the hand of the partner.

MEDIO CONTRADA, MEDIUM RANGE

At that range it is possible to touch the body of the opponent with the weapon, but not yet with the natural weapons (feet, fists,…).

It is a relevant range for the work with the single stick (Solo Baston). The strikes are less powerful than at Largo Mano, but fast and less readable. The defenses with blockings are more conceivable.

While training, to check that they do stand at Medio Contrada range, the two partners are facing each other in fighting stance, arm stretched, stick stretched. The last 4 inches of the stick must touch the shoulder of the partner.

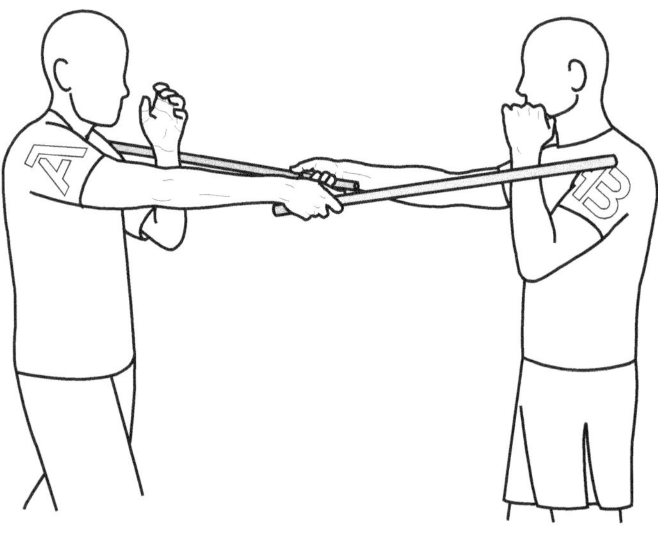

Corto, Short Range

At that range it is possible to touch the body of the opponent with the natural weapons.

With a stick, strikes with the punyo or in Abaniko are particularly efficient. The stick may be used for locks and controls.

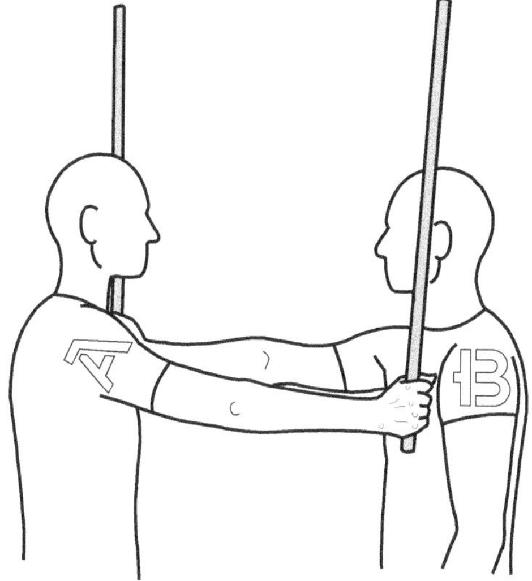

II. Footworks

It will never be repeated enough, whatever the martial art, that it uses hands, feet (knees, elbows, head,…) impacts or weapons, the footwork is primordial.

We move to enter in a combat range, to dodge, to get out of the line of attack, to support a strike or a control technique, to change opponent… and, of course, to leave the fight.

Mobility is essential.

To learn how to move is: to have at our disposal an array of maneuvers, and to be able to use them appropriately and to perform them with proper timing. But more importantly we must keep our balance and our structure, as well as our guard, in order to maximize the availability of the whole body at both within the move and after. For the fighter, and moreover the Eskrima practitioner (the eskrimador), as the chess player, is both at what he is doing and at the following moves…

In a first step, we can isolate 'the footwork' to teach it, and maybe exercise it in a dynamic way as a specific warm-up.

In this chapter the different footworks are presented with this idea — from a neutral starting position from which we can work to the left and to the right with several repetitions.

It is repetition that allows the footwork to become 'natural' (acquired), flowing and efficient, and so allows the eskrimador to effectively execute it in his training with weapons, then eventually under stress in a real fight.

These footworks will be found, quite logically, within the exercises and applications described all over the book.

FEMALE TRIANGLE

The concept of the triangle is omnipresent in Filipino Martial Arts. That explains that so many schools around the world use this geometrical shape in their logos.
Seen from the top, the Abierta and Serrada guards both form a triangle.

For the exercise, it is pretty easy to mark out the triangle by putting two sticks on the floor. The eskrimadors who have their own training room can also paint the geometrical shape on the floor.

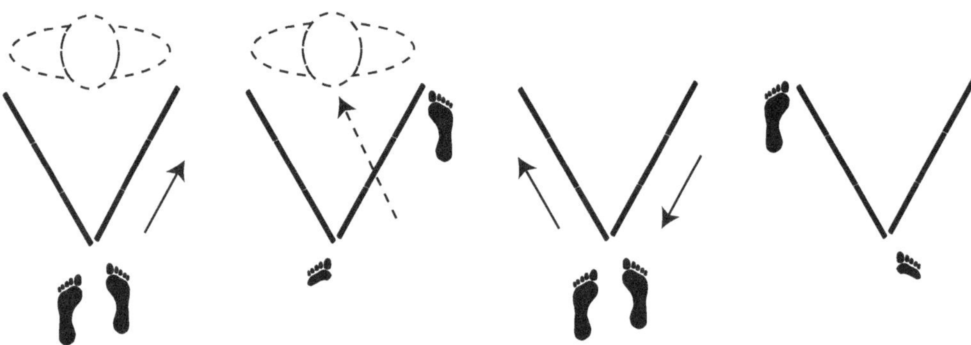

For the 'female' triangle footwork, the eskrimador stands, feet together, at the tip of the triangle. We can imagine that the opponent stands on the opposite base. In order not to neglect a correct body structure, a guard with the hands held high must be maintain. It is not appropriate to work with the arms dangled.

The footwork to the right is performed by placing the right foot on the right tip of the triangle. The left foot, that thus became 'the back foot', has its heel lift away from the floor. Simultaneously, we rotate the pelvis to keep the position of the adversary in our line. Then we comes back to the central tip, feet together.
The footwork to the left is exactly the same as the right one, but as a mirror image.

To train the footwork in a dynamic way, we can do right and left sequentially, each time going through the central position.
To the next level of the exercise, once the hand skills are acquired, we can add to the footwork a simultaneous sequence of strikes to execute with each step, with a return to a guard when stepping back to the center.

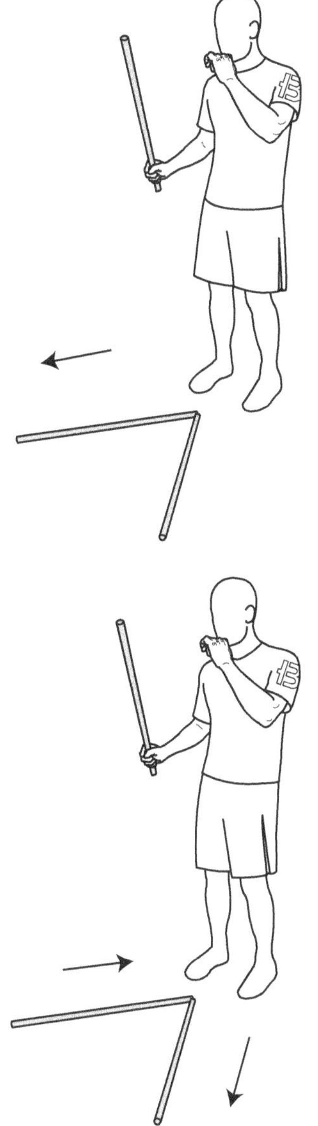

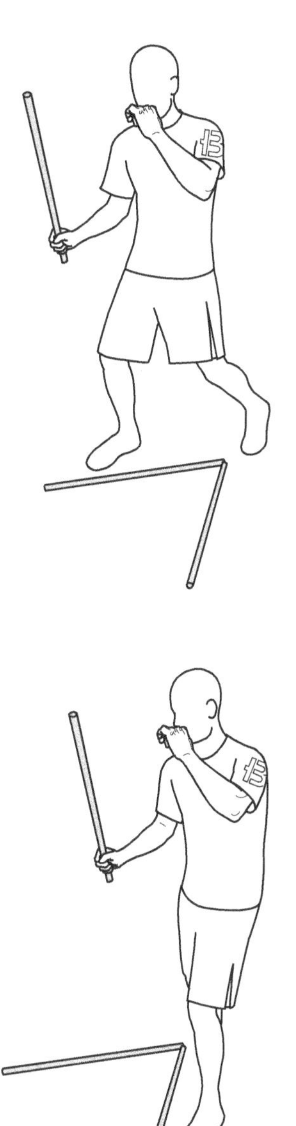

EXAMPLE:

Feet together at the tip of the triangle in Abierta guard
Triangle footwork to the right
Do angle 2 Lobtik after angle 1 Lobtik (being careful to work on a virtual opponent standing on the base of the triangle)
Return with feet together to the tip of the triangle (in Abierta guard)
Triangle footwork to the left
Do angle 1 Lobtik after angle 2 Lobtik
Return...

Female Triangle 2

The eskrimador stands, feet together, at the tip of the triangle. As for the previous footwork, he places his right foot at the right tip of the triangle. The weight of the body is on that leg. That allows to move the left foot to the left tip, passing by the right tip, while always keeping his balance. In practice, the left leg has made a circle arc. The right foot goes back to the starting point, then the left one.

The footwork to the right is done several times, then the left one is done. The footwork to the left is the exact mirror image of the right one.

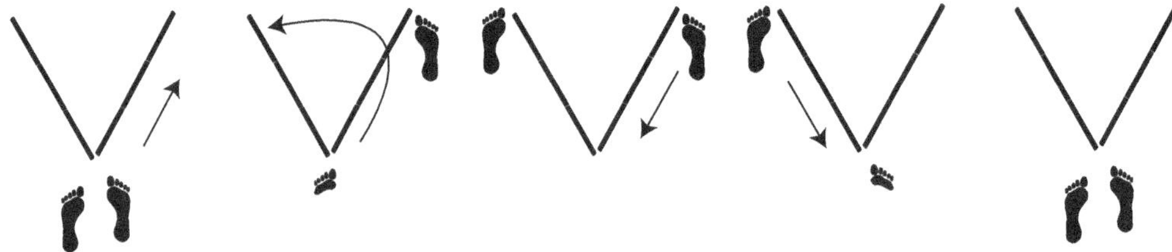

Male Triangle

The eskrimador stands, feet together, at the tip of the triangle, back to the base. He puts his right foot to the right tip. He returns feet together to the central tip, and then puts his left foot to the left tip. With several repetitions, to train the footwork.

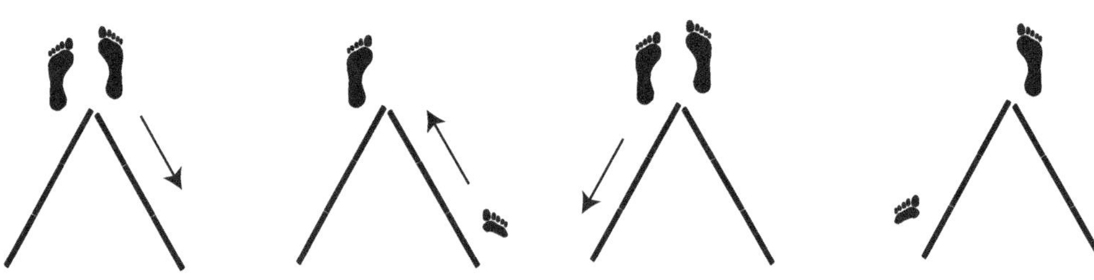

In an unrestricted work, we can imagine two identical triangles joined together by their tips, like the shape of an hourglass, or an x-cross. The eskrimador stands in the center, feet together, and links Female Triangles and Male Triangles, while going through the center each time. He is careful of his physical attitude. He works in a flowing and relaxed way. He keeps his balance, ensures his shifting of weight, and maintain his gaze wide open and his hands raised in guard (bare hands or armed, it must not collapse).

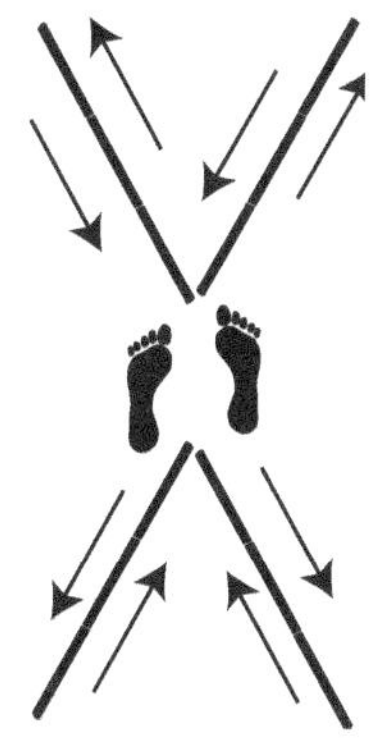

Male Triangle 2

The eskrimador stands feet lined up on the base of the triangle, shoulder-width apart. He puts his right foot on the tip of the triangle. From a neutral position, he stepped in his fighting stance, weight of the body mainly shifted on the forward leg, the right foot flat, the left foot with its heel lift away from the floor.

To train the footwork, he steps back the right foot to its initial position, then repeat the movement with his left foot.

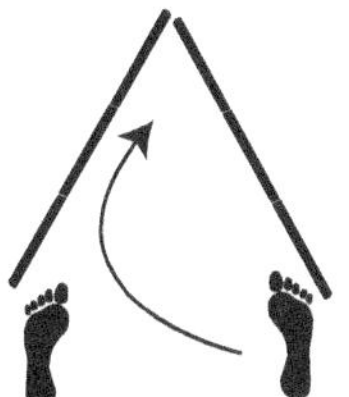  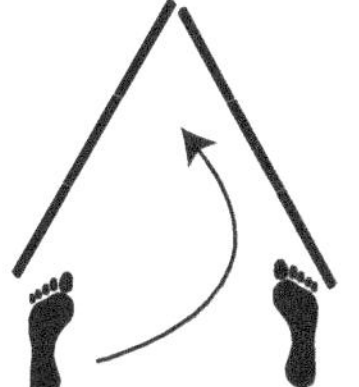 

DIAMOND

We visualize the shape of a diamond, or two triangles joined at their bases. The eskrimador stands, feet together, at the tip of the diamond. As for the triangle footwork, he puts his right foot on the right tip of the diamond. Then his left foot comes to join his right foot, before continuing its way to the opposite tip.

To return to the initial point, he steps back his left foot, passing by the position of the right foot. Then steps back in turn the right foot, to be feet together. The footwork to the left is the mirror image.

In order to train this footwork in a dynamic way, the right and the left sides of the diamond are covered one after the other, each time going through the initial tip.

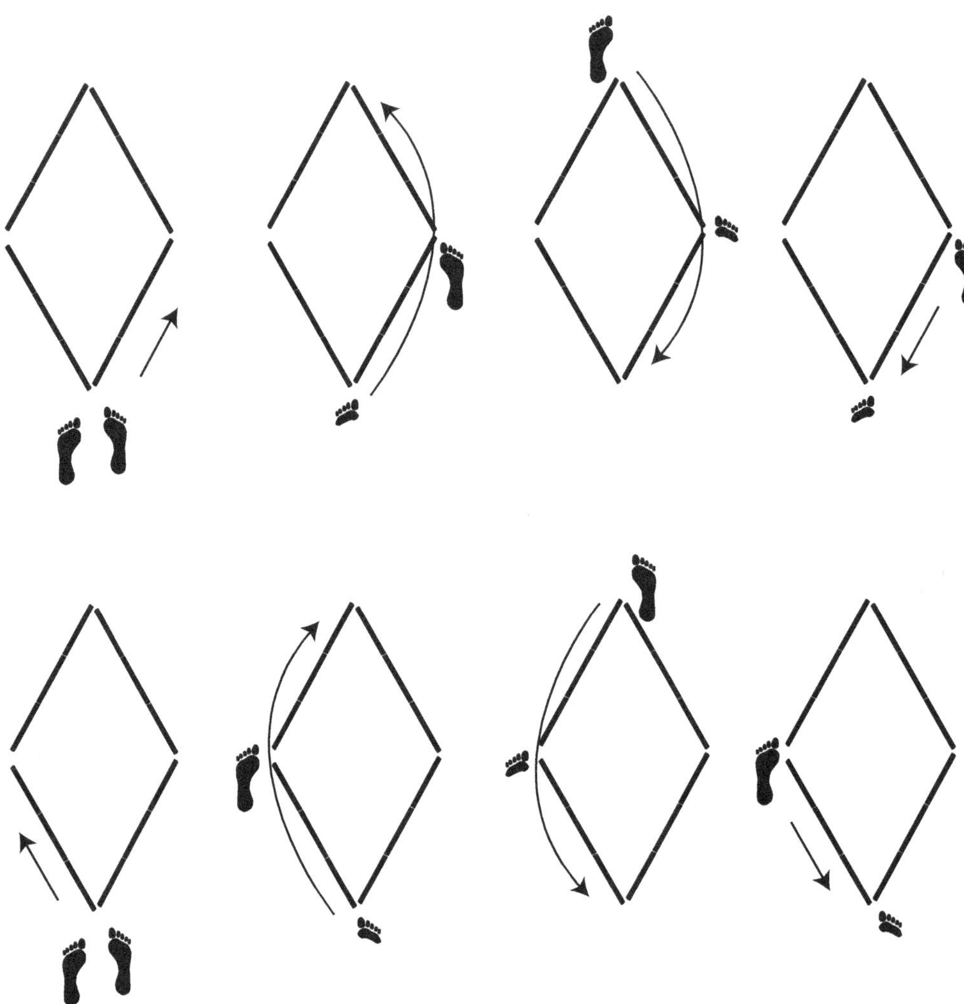

FEMALE TRIANGLE AND STEP ASIDE

While doing this movement, a female triangle footwork is done then the back foot is shifted aside, which redirects the body.

In practice, that movement allows to get out of the line of attack of the adversary (notably when facing a forward thrust or a charge), while staying away and keeping the opponent in our own line of attack.

In a dynamic training of the footwork, when the movement has been done to the right, step back to the central tip and then do the footwork to the left…

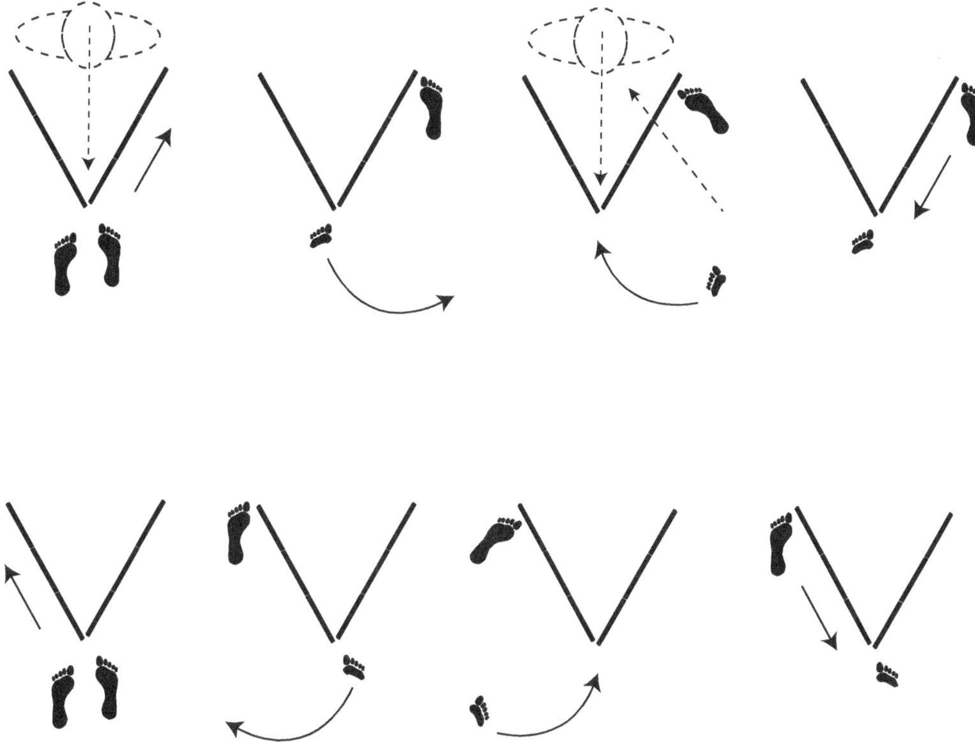

STEP ASIDE

Feet shoulder-width apart. One foot steps aside in a backward circular move. Body mechanics makes the torso rotate and get it out of the line of attack of a forward thrust. Nevertheless it is important to keep the intention directed to the opponent position.

For the dynamic training of the footwork: return in the initial position, and step aside with the other leg.

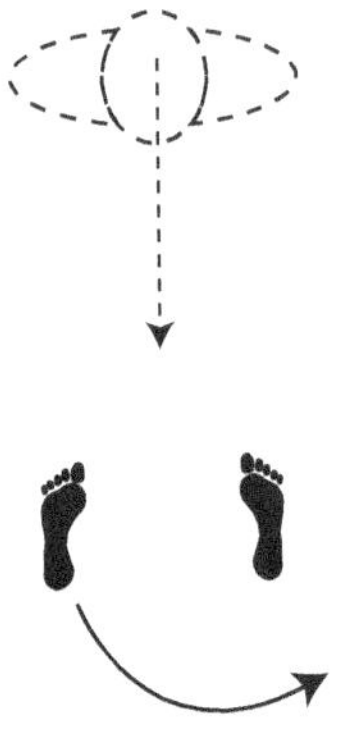 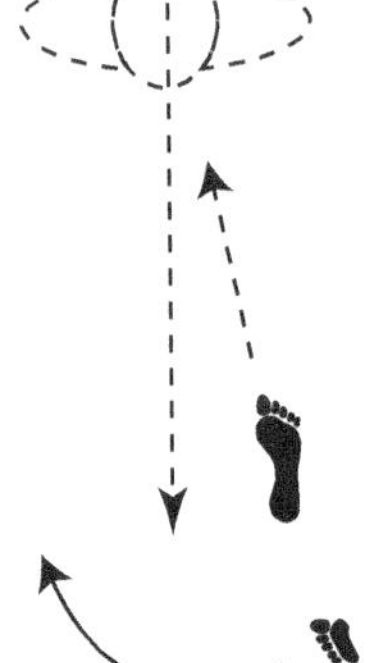  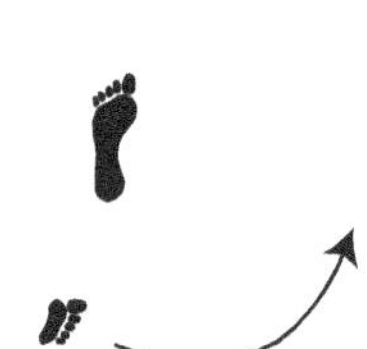

PIVOT ON THE BALLS OF FEET

Feet shoulder-width apart. We pivot to the right then to the left by lifting our heels from the floor and shifting our weight.

CROSSED FOOTWORK

Feet shoulder-width apart. To move to the right, the left leg passes in front of the right leg. The legs are then crossed. To uncross, the right foot is shifted to the right while changing the orientation of the body to face the opponent.

The footwork to the left is the exact mirror image of the right one.

We can use this crossed / uncrossed footwork to move around a circle.

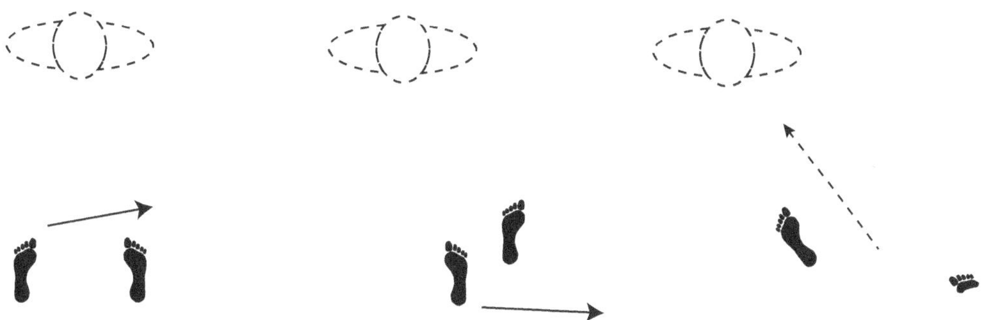

STANCE SWITCH

Start in fighting stance, feet shoulder-width apart, right foot forward and flat on the floor, heel of the rearward foot lifted up.

Bring the left foot at the level of the right foot, and step back the right foot, without covering any distance. Adapt the hands guard, following the principle 'same foot / same hand' (when the right foot is forward, the right hand is forward).

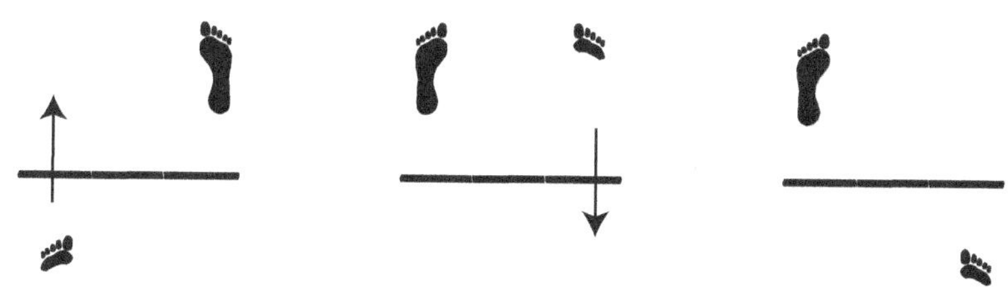

RETIRADA ILUSTRISIMO / THE STEP

Retirada, that sounds like 'retreat', is a footwork that allows, in an offensive way, to quickly enter a range and then get out of it, and similarly, in a defensive way, to quickly step back and then step forward.

Alternatively, the two Retirada footworks described in this section can be used to move forward or to move backward while maintaining a good fighting attitude and physical structure.

Start in fighting stance, feet shoulder-width apart, right foot forward and flat on the floor, heel of the rearward foot lifted up. The left foot steps forward like we do an usual walking step. It becomes the forward foot, flat on the floor, and the right foot becomes the rearward foot, heel lifted up from the floor.

For dynamic training, do several repetitions (forward and backward), and switch stances from time to time to train both sides.

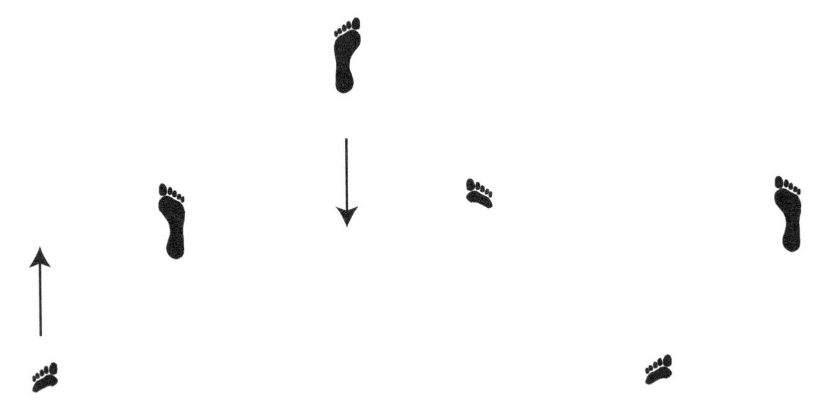

RETIRADA CABALLERO / THE HALF-STEP

Sometimes called the 'shuffle step', the half-step allows to move forward or move backward without switching stance. Contrary to what one might think, the distance covered is not the half of a step. We can make a very little half-step to slightly correct a range, or make a wide half step to suddenly fill a gap.

Start in fighting stance, feet shoulder-width apart, right foot forward and flat on the floor, heel of the rearward foot lifted up.
To move forward, the right foot steps away from the left foot. The left foot immediately corrects the distance to maintain balance and structure. Although it is the right foot that initiates the footwork, the impulse generated by the ball of the

rearward foot is not to be neglected. The rearward foot does not 'lag behind'.

To move backward, the left foot steps away from the right foot, and this one corrects immediately the created gap.

Of course, it is to be trained on both stances.

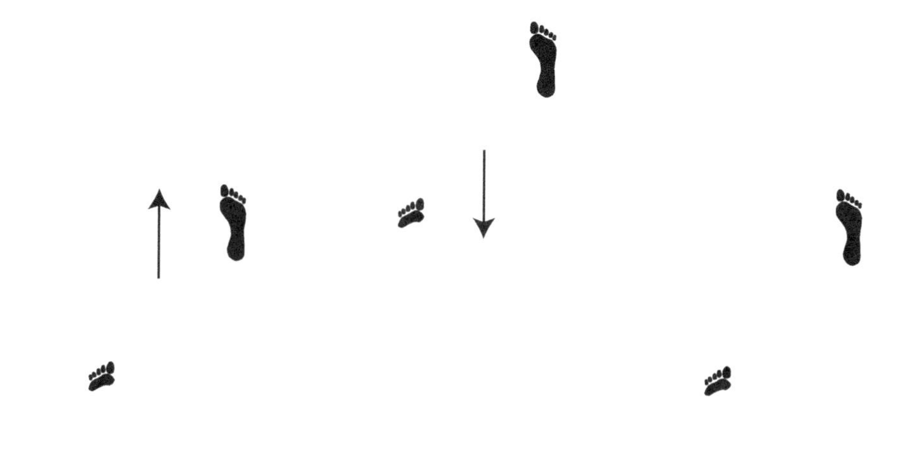

PIVOT

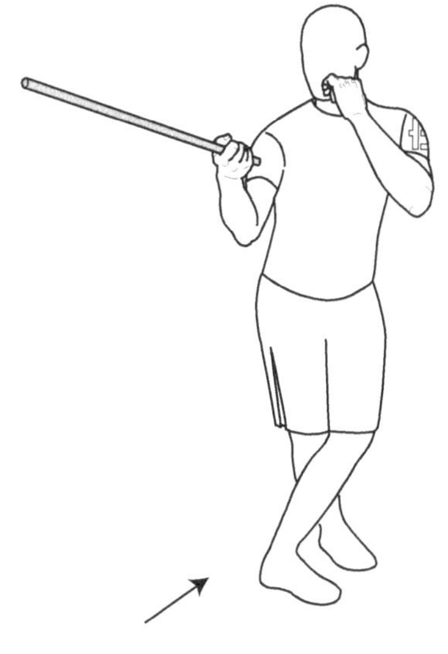

Starting in fighting stance, the eskrimador draws back his forward leg, similarly to a Retirada Ilustrisimo, while pivoting his rearward foot. He then stands himself, for a split second, legs crossed, knee into hollow of the knee, before stepping back forward. The intention stays focused forward.

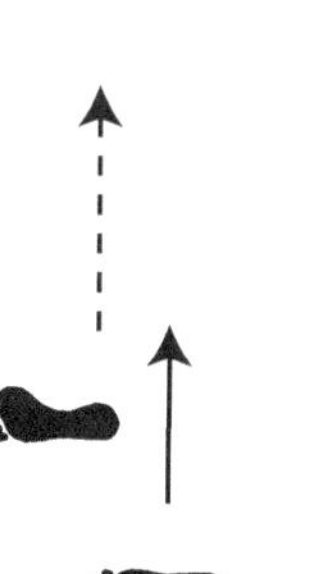

III. BODY MOBILITY

Or the art of moving without stepping... We have seen previously that the footwork is important to change the combat range, or to maximize the efficiency of a technique. In Eskrima, two movements of the body are also essential to reach these goals.

ELASTIKO

In an offensive way at Largo Mano, there are two options to get contact with the trunk of the opponent :
— to move with a Retirada, which allows to enter in the range and get back.
— remain on the same spot but exaggerate the body mechanics to stretch and reach the range, while standing firm on your feet. It is Elastiko.

The same can be done in a defensive way, by dodging backward with the chest while standing firm on your position for example. And of course we can combine Elastiko with a footwork.

TORQUE

The teaching of many martial arts and combat sports, including boxing, emphasizes the importance of being relaxed and the use of the hip rotation movement to develop proper power.

It is the same for Eskrima. The sole movement of the wrist and the arm allows only to achieve limited power. The proper striking (or cutting) power is only achieved with the coordination of the whole body: the foundations of the legs, the rotation of the hip — the Torque — and finally the shoulder and the arm.

Relaxation and coordination are the important words. The Torque can be more or less emphasized according to the desired effect, but it must be done with these two words in mind to become a significant ally of your efficiency.

Solo Baston

I. Numerado

Classical Numerado

A stick held in the right hand, in fighting stance and Abierta guard, the eskrimador executes in sequence the nine basic strikes. He thus familiarizes himself with the angles and the handling of the stick. Although it is a blunt weapon, it is important to train with the idea of cutting.

When we are at ease and the movements begin to sequence in a flow, the footwork is added. Here, a Retirada (a Step) is done simultaneously to the execution of certain angles:

From the right stance (right foot forward) Abierta
Angle 1 Lobtik
Angle 2 Lobtik the left foot stepping forward
Angle 3 Lobtik the left foot stepping backward
Angle 4 Lobtik the left foot stepping forward
Angle 5 stepping the left foot backward
Angle 6 Lobtik the left foot stepping forward
Angle 7 Lobtik the left foot stepping backward
Angle 8
Angle 9

This exercise, that is first done alone in the air, can also be trained with a partner as we will see in the section about Drills.

AHUAPAN NUMERADO

It is a variation of the classical numerado that consists of a sequence of 14 movements.

To do it as a loop exercise, it only takes to step forward after the last movement and execute again the angle 1 strike (first move).

It is also interesting to do this exercise with the stick held in the left hand, while adapting the stance and the footwork.

Front right stance Abierta
Angle 1 Lobtik

Angle 4 Lobtik
the left foot stepping forward

Angle 3 Lobtik
the left foot
stepping backward

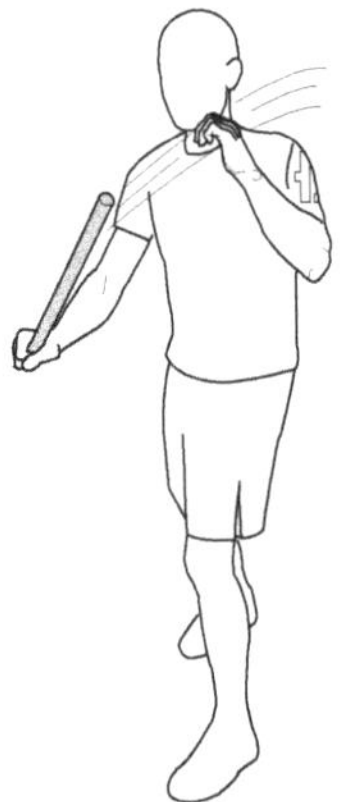

Angle 2 Lobtik
the left foot stepping forward

Angle 5
the left foot
stepping backward

Angle 9

Angle 8

Angle 6 Lobtik
the left foot stepping forward

Angle 7 Lobtik
the left foot
stepping backward

Abaniko
to the left temple

Abaniko
to the right temple

Redondo

Punyo to the face
the left foot stepping forward

Kurbada while making two
steps backward

II. Basic Counters & Check

We train with a partner, at Medio Contrada range (arm stretched, stick stretched, we can touch the body of the partner). The two partners hold a stick in the right hand.

Training with partners

When we train with one or more partners, there is no need to rush and strike quickly and hard to get a proper dynamic of training.

Some might feel this as a lack of 'realism'. But confidence, in ourselves and between partners, must be built before speed and force are increased. Moreover, the quality of the movement must be prioritized before power.

A controlled speed of training allows to make contact without danger, except for direct strikes to the head where an additional caution will be apllied (or appropriate protections); it is the benefit of training with a stick. At that speed an impact is only a minor discomfort to the partner. It is especially important not to try to stop the blow before the target, or worse, to deliberately miss the target. The body, the eye or the brain tend to record these 'wrong ranges' and restitute them.

With practice, the two partners will get confidence and technical quality. They also get used to impacts. They can be more 'playful' with each other. And if they look for 'stronger' exchanges, they can equip themselves with protections.

For all the exercises (counters, drills, disarms, applications...) described hereafter we assume that A and B are right-handed, and will naturally use the weapon in their main hand. Of course it is preferable, or even recommended, to train also each exercise, with the necessary adaptations, while partners hold their stick in their left hand. First because a part of the eskrimadors are left-handed, but also to enhance their ambidexterity, their ease with both hands, and prepare to a possible injury that would incapacitate the main hand.

ANGLE 1 COUNTER

A serves an angle 1 strike
B interposes his stick, forming a cross with the stick of A. Care must be taken to ensure that the contact point is in the center of the stick of A.

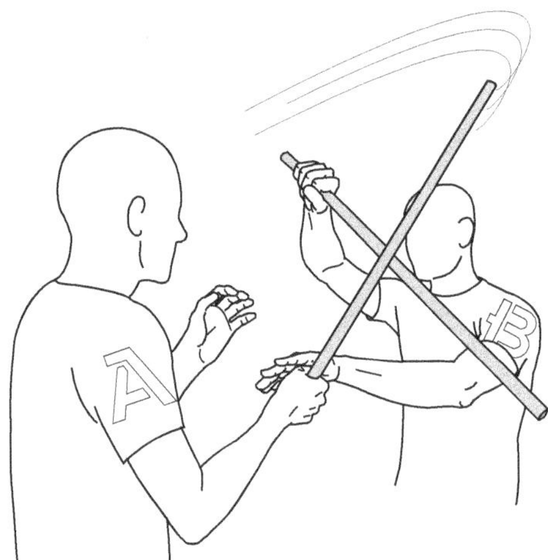

This defensive move can be done with the tip towards the floor (Wing or Roof Block) or the tip towards the ceiling (Inside Sweep).

The inertia of the moving stick of A is greater than that of the stick of B. So it is appropriate to add a secondary contact point to support the defense. In that purpose the 'Check' is used.

B makes the Check with his unarmed hand. That maneuver consists actually in 'checking' by hand contact, more specifically in controlling the position of the hand of the opponent.

In the defense, while B interposes his stick between the strike of A, he places (with a slight delay, like an half beat in music) his unarmed hand on the armed hand of A. Thus he establishes a secondary contact point with the attack. But the Check will also allow him to anticipate the next move of the weapon of A or to make a control maneuver (see the section on Disarms).

If B has made his counter with the tip towards the ceiling, he will place his Check from below. On the contrary, if he has made his counter with the tip towards the floor, he will place his Check from above.

ANGLE 2 COUNTER

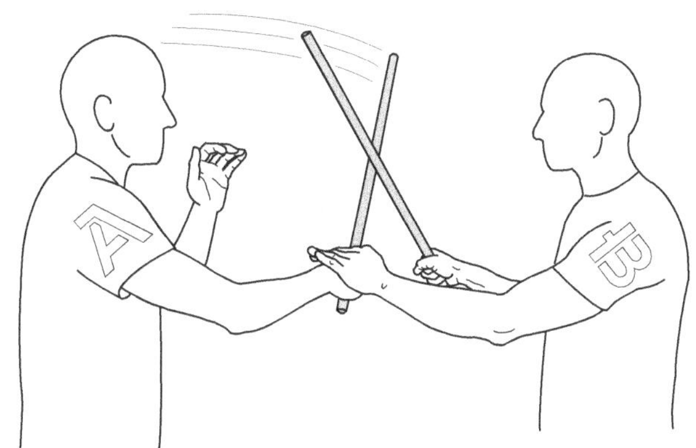

A serves an angle 2 strike
B interposes his stick, tip towards the ceiling, and checks.

Basic Counters

ANGLE 3 COUNTER

A serves an angle 3 strike
B interposes his stick and checks. That maneuver can be done tip towards the floor, or towards the ceiling.

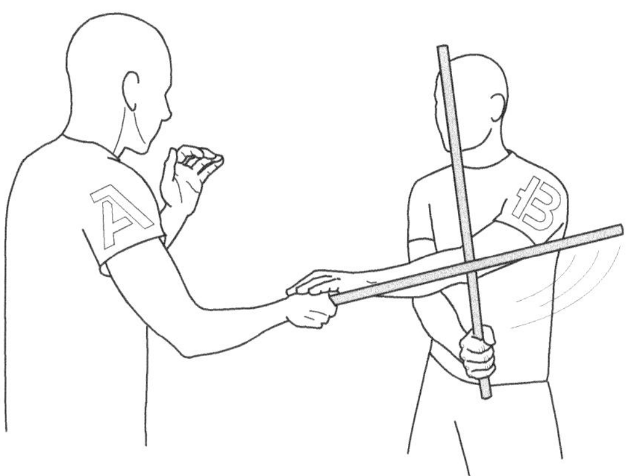

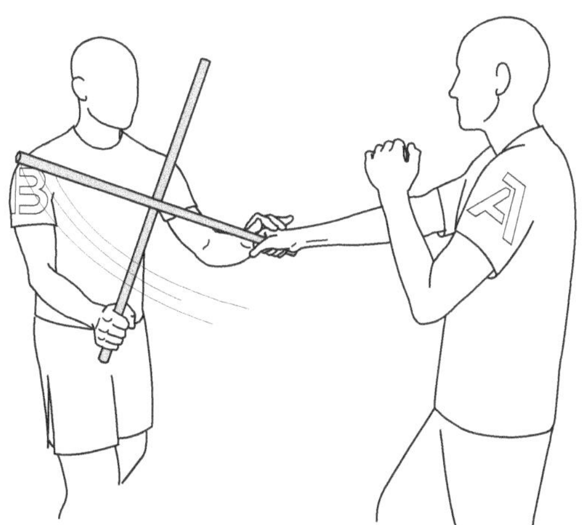

ANGLE 4 COUNTER

A serves an angle 4 strike
B interposes his stick and checks tip towards the ceiling.

ANGLE 5 COUNTER

A serves an angle 5 thrust
B does a step aside (see chapter on the footworks) while making contact with his stick and the one of A (it is not a blocking), and checks with his unarmed hand.

The step aside can be inside or outside, and the contact with the stick with the tip towards the ceiling or towards the floor.

If B has no time to step aside he must, as a minimum, use his body mobility to move away the targets (as a matter of fact his abdomen) from the line of attack.

ANGLE 6 COUNTER

A serves an angle 6 strike
B steps away his right leg and interposes his stick, as if he was going to stick it into the ground, and checks.

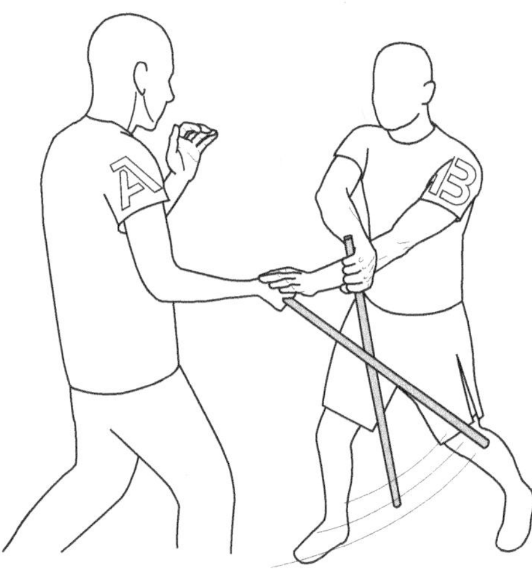

ANGLE 7 COUNTER

A serves an angle 7 strike
B interposes his stick, as if he was going to stick it into the ground, and checks.

BLOCKING DRILLS: EXERCISES WITH PARTNER USING NUMERADO AND BASIC COUNTERS

To boost the training of basic counters, we can propose several exercises:

EXERCISE 1

Medio Contrada range
A serves angles 1 to 7
B does the appropriate counters
B serves angles 1 to 7
A does the appropriate counters
…

EXERCISE 2 :

Medio Contrada range
A serves angle 1 / B counters
B serves angle 1 / A counters
A serves angle 2 / B counters
B serves angle 2 / A counters
A serves angle 3 /…

EXERCISE 3 :

Medio Contrada range
A serves angle 1 / B counters
B serves angle 2 / A counters
A serves angle 3 / B counters
B serves angle 4 / A counters
A serves angle 5 / B counters
B serves angle 6 / A counters
A serves angle 7 / B counters
B serves angle 1 /…

EXERCISE 4 :

Keeping this principle of 'your turn / my turn', and using the seven angles of strike and the basic counters, the partners may now be free to choose the angle of their blow (among the seven options) when their turn comes.

III. Drills

While teaching Filipino Martial Arts, we often use pedagogic exercises for two people in loops — sequences of maneuvers repeated several times, where will be introduced afterwards variations or finalizations. These are the Drills.

The purpose of a drill is to develop certain martial attributes (coordination, estimation of distances, etc...), and particularly reactions conditioned by the repetition, some sort of 'educated reflexes'. To achieve that the two partners training the drill must be able to run it in loops several times without error.

As it is very difficult to correct a bad habit, it is important to pay attention to the details when doing a drill, in order to nurture the proper move and not the error. For example, we check that our angle of strike his correctly aimed to the target (a part of the body of the partner) and not towards the stick of the partner (like children playing to be knights...).

Similarly, the repetitive side of the drill is in itself a default. Once the difficulty of learning the angles and the movements is overcome, and the partners are at ease, they tend to turn their minds elsewhere while doing the drill, as there is no need anymore to focus. It is the time to introduce in the training some variations. And so, the necessity to focus is there again.

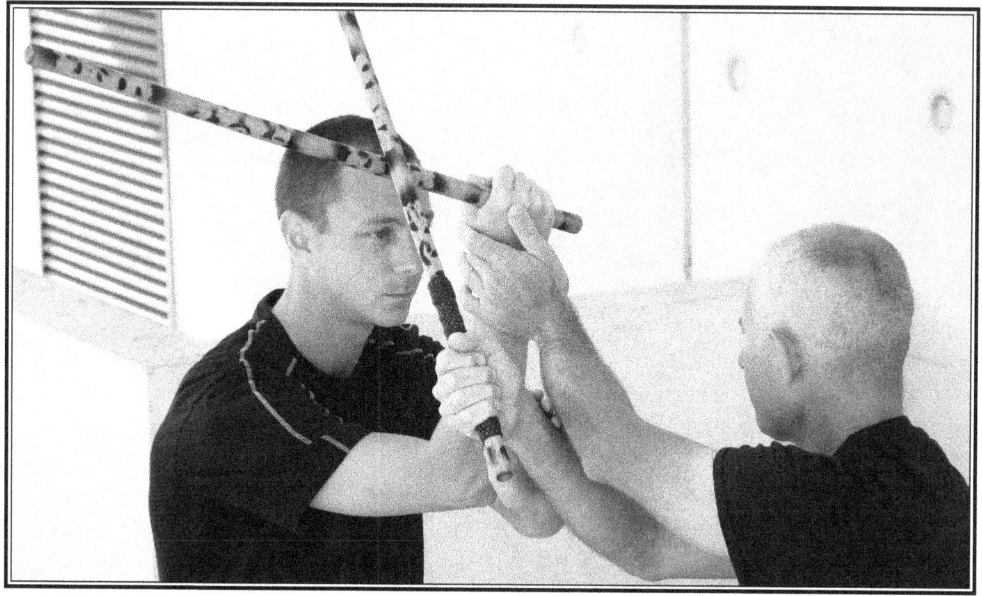

NUMERADO — ABECEDARIO

Largo Mano range, Abierta right stance
A and B serve simultaneously the numerado from 1 to 9
For the angles 3 and 4, give a slight inclination to the sticks in order to make contact
Angle 5, A and B step forward with the left foot and deflect the thrust outside with the palm of their unarmed hand
Angle 6, step back the left foot to go back to Largo Mano
Angle 8, A and B step forward with the left foot and deflect the thrust outside with the palm of their unarmed hand
Angle 9, A and B deflect the thrust inside with the palm of their unarmed hand
Step back the left foot, while the stick is passed behind the head, and back to Largo Mano range

The two partners do the drill again from the beginning. The first goal will be to be able to do it several times without hesitations and mistakes.

HIGH LOW HIGH

Largo Mano range, Abierta right stance
Angle 1 Lobtik
Angle 6 Witik
Angle 2 Lobtik

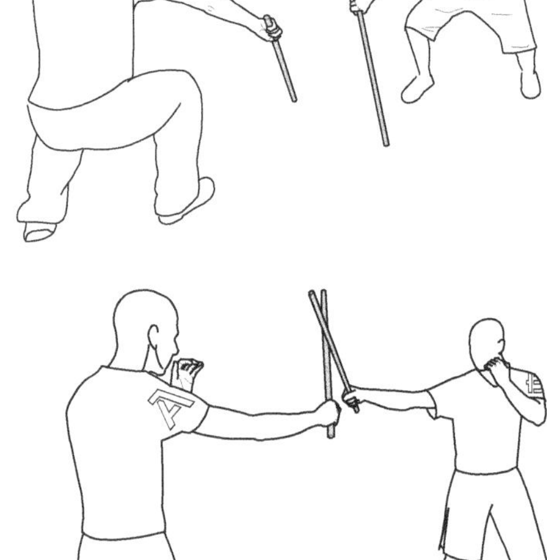

4 COUNT

The initial pattern of the drill is the same as High Low High, one movement is added.

Largo Mano range, Abierta right stance
Angle 1 Lobtik
Angle 6 Witik
Angle 2 Lobtik
Angle 7 Witik

TRES TRES

Medio Contrada range, Abierta right stance
A lowers his stand and serves an angle 3 Lobtik at thigh level
B lowers his stand and counters with the tip towards the floor
B serves angle 4 Lobtik
A counters with the tip towards the floor (wing)
A stands up and serves a descending vertical strike to the head
B counters with a Roof Block
B lowers his stand and serves an angle 3 Lobtik at thigh level…

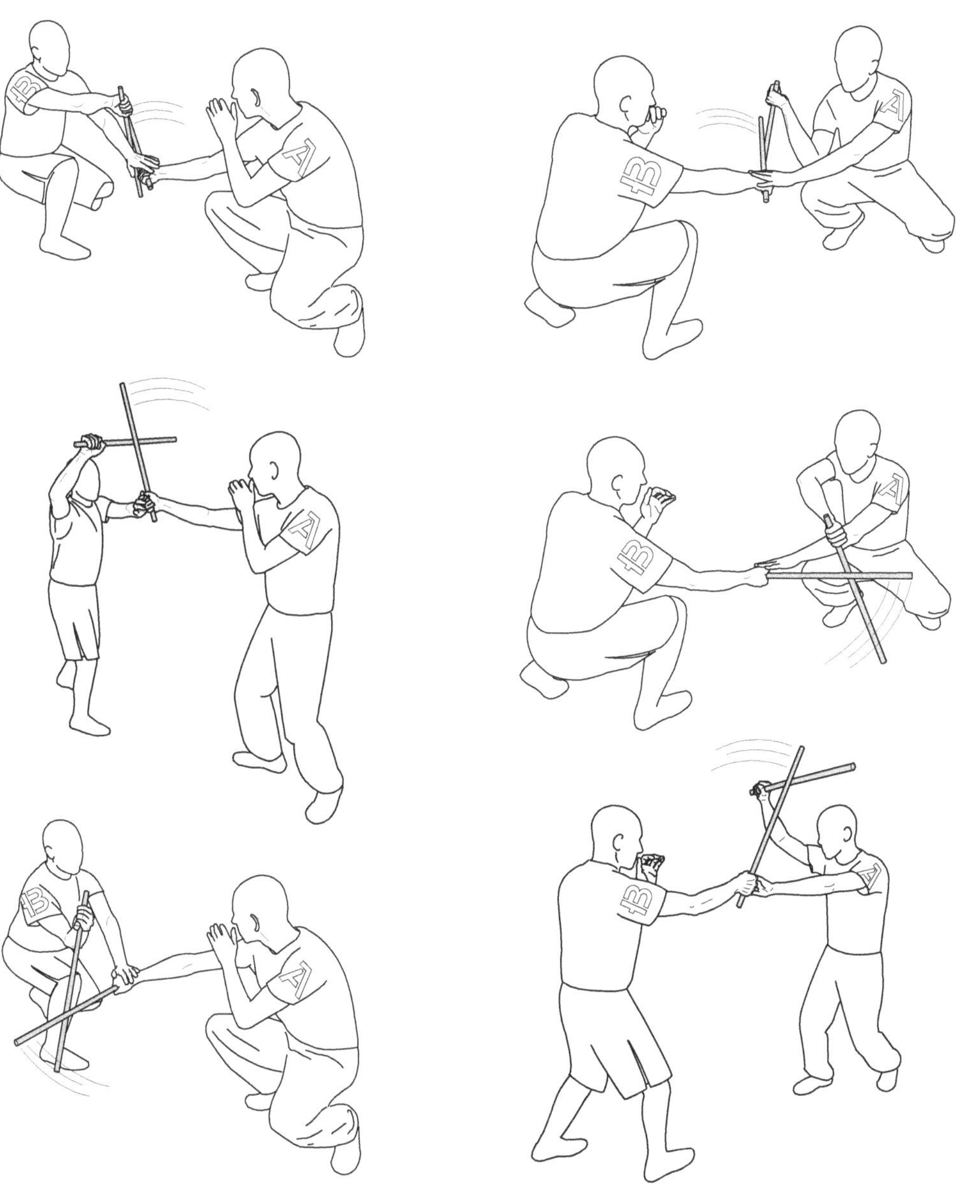

BOX DRILL

Box Drill is an exercise common to many schools of Eskrima.

Its pattern teaches the logic of the most appropriate move and so the fastest to apply. The attacks are delivered where the way is open. The defenses depend on the position of the stick at the moment of the attack.

It is also an excellent exercise to train the Check, perfectly suited to Medio Contrada range. Each time he defends, the eskrimador does a Check.

Medio Contrada range, Abierta right stance
A serves angle 1 Lobtik
B counters, tip towards the floor, and checks
B passes his stick behind his head and serves angle 1 Lobtik
A counters, tip towards the ceiling, and checks
A serves angle 4 Lobtik
B counters with a dissolution (strike to the stick of A) supported by his Check
B, using the rebound of his stick, serves angle 1 Lobtik
A counters, tip towards the floor, and checks
A passes his stick behind his head and serves angle 1 Lobtik
B counters, tip towards the ceiling, and checks
B serves angle 4 Lobtik
A counters with a dissolution supported by his Check
A serves angle 1…

SUMBRADA 5

It is a 'your turn / my turn' drill in five moves. Some of them are common with Box Drill.

In the version hereafter, we have deliberately inserted a sixth facultative move, a strike with the Punyo, that makes a link with the following drill, Punyo Sumbrada.

Medio Contrada range, Abierta right stance
A serves angle 1 Lobtik
B counters, tip towards the ceiling, and checks
B serves angle 4 Lobtik
A counters with a dissolution
A serves an angle 5 thrust
B counters, tip towards the floor, and checks
B serves a thrust with the Punyo to the face
A blocks with his unarmed hand at the level of the forearm of B
B serves a vertical Abaniko strike to the head
A counters with a Roof Block, with his elbow inside
With his unarmed hand, A pushes aside the arm of B and serves a descending strike to the head
B quickly steps aside with a triangle footwork while protecting himself with his stick (Umbrella)
B passes his stick behind his head and serves angle 1 Lobtik
A counters, tip towards the ceiling, and checks
A serves angle 4…

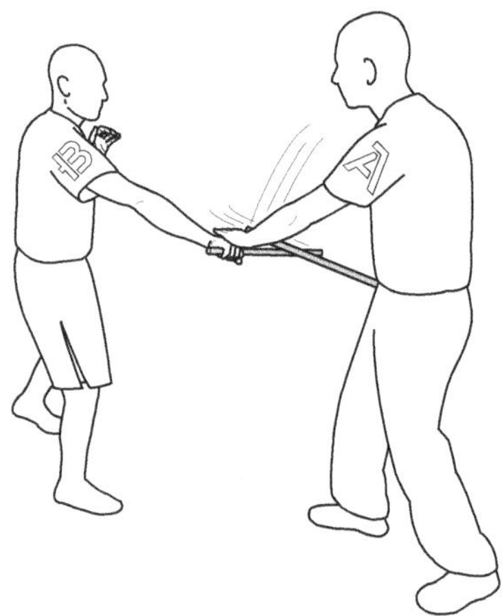

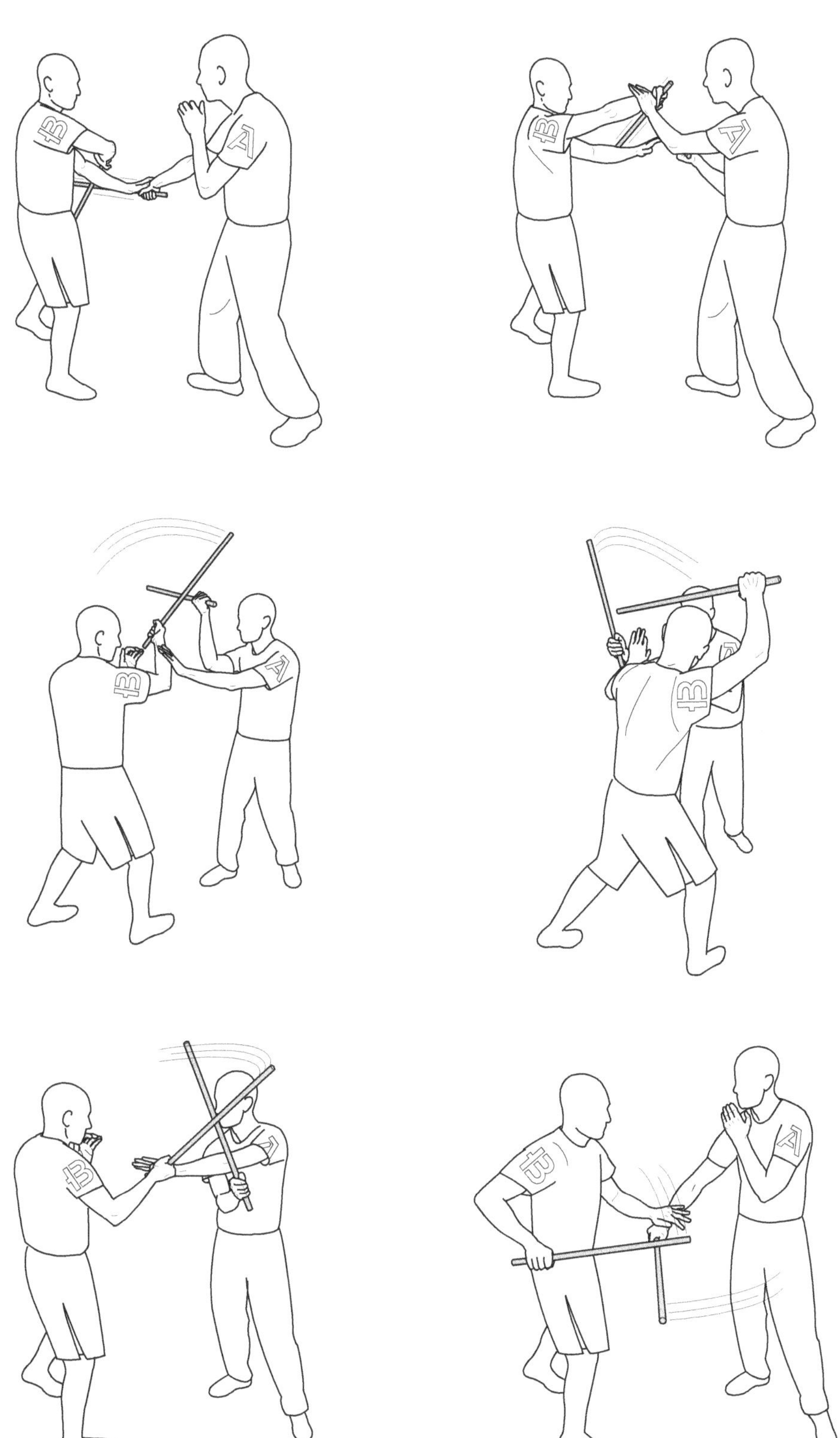

PUNYO SUMBRADA

Corto range, Abierta right stance
A serves angle 3 Lobtik (or, as a variation, an angle 5 thrust as in Sumbrada 5)
B counters, tip towards the floor, and checks
B serves a thrust with the Punyo to the face
A blocks with his unarmed hand at the level of the forearm of B
B serves a vertical Abaniko strike to the head
A counters with a Roof Block, with his elbow inside
B moves his unarmed hand in the rectangle formed by the sticks and the forearm of A, and controls the arm of A clockwise
In the movement B serves an angle 6 to the stick of A — in combat, it is a strike with the Punyo on the armed hand of A
B serves angle 3 Lobtik
A counters, tip towards the floor, and checks
A serves a thrust with the Punyo to the face
B blocks with his unarmed hand…

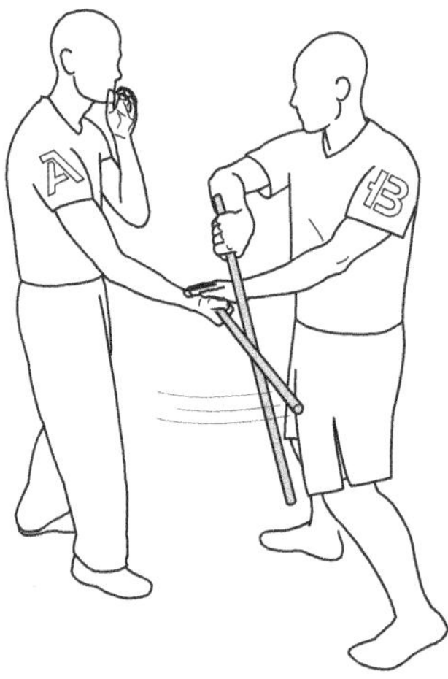

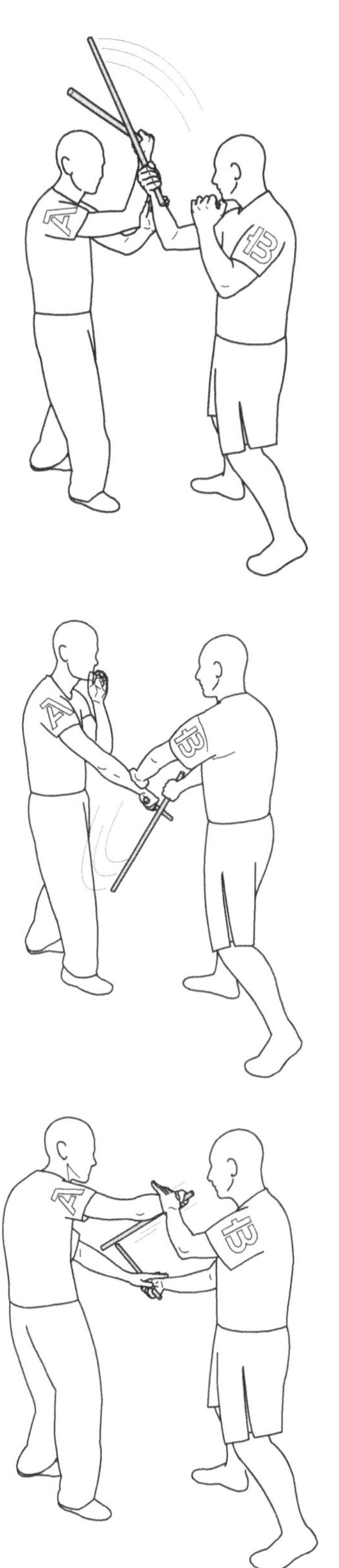

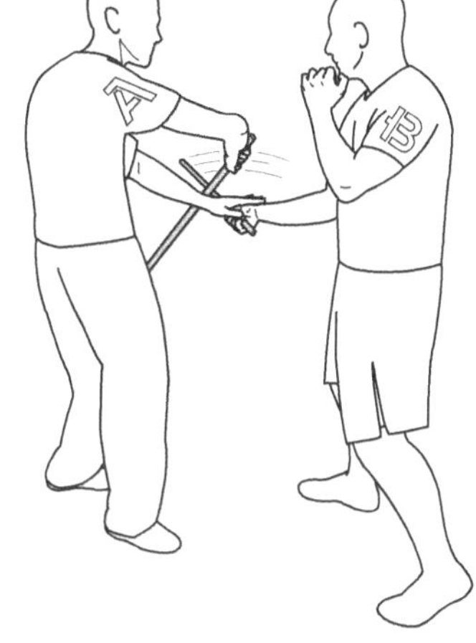

Hubud Lubud

The very popular drill of Hubud Lubud can be done with sticks, with knives and with bare hands. Its working distance and the development of sensitivity it induces, are the reason why it is often compared to Chi Sao in Wing Chun, or Tui Shou in Tai Chi. The version with sticks, Solo Baston, is presented hereafter.

Corto range, Abierta right stance
1. A serves an angle 1 Punyo strike
B counters with his unarmed arm at the level of the wrist while he rotates his torso to absorb the attack and move away the target. It is necessary to face the vector of attack.
2. B serves a vertical Abaniko strike to the the stick of A — in combat, it is a strike with the Punyo, or an Abaniko, to the armed hand of A — then he places his forearm under the forearm of A, thus establishing a new control to free his unarmed hand
3. B puts his unarmed hand on the outside of the armed arm of A, just above the elbow joint, and push it away clockwise
1. B serves an angle 1 Punyo strike
A counters with his unarmed arm…

A first variation that can be brought in this drill is to offer a 'gift', a strike, to the partner without breaking the rhythm of the drill.

For example, between move 1 and 2, B can do a vertical Abaniko strike to the right foot of A or an angle 4 strike in the ribs.

Other example, while doing move 3, as he moves his stick from the left to the right, B can deliver an horizontal Abaniko strike to the side of the head of A.

These gifts must not be done at each loop of the drill, but offered from time to time by one or the other partner throughout the course of the exercise.

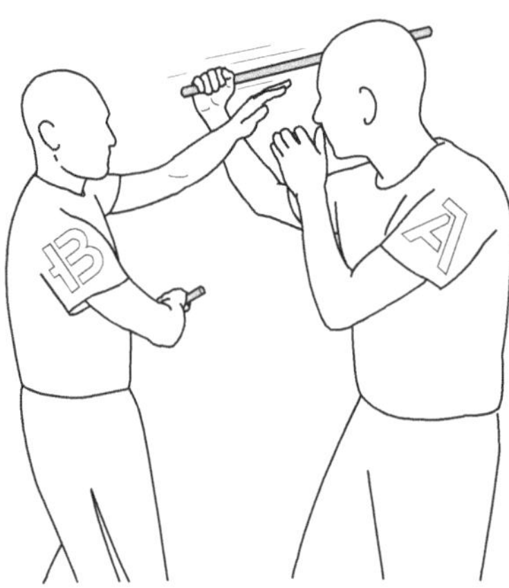

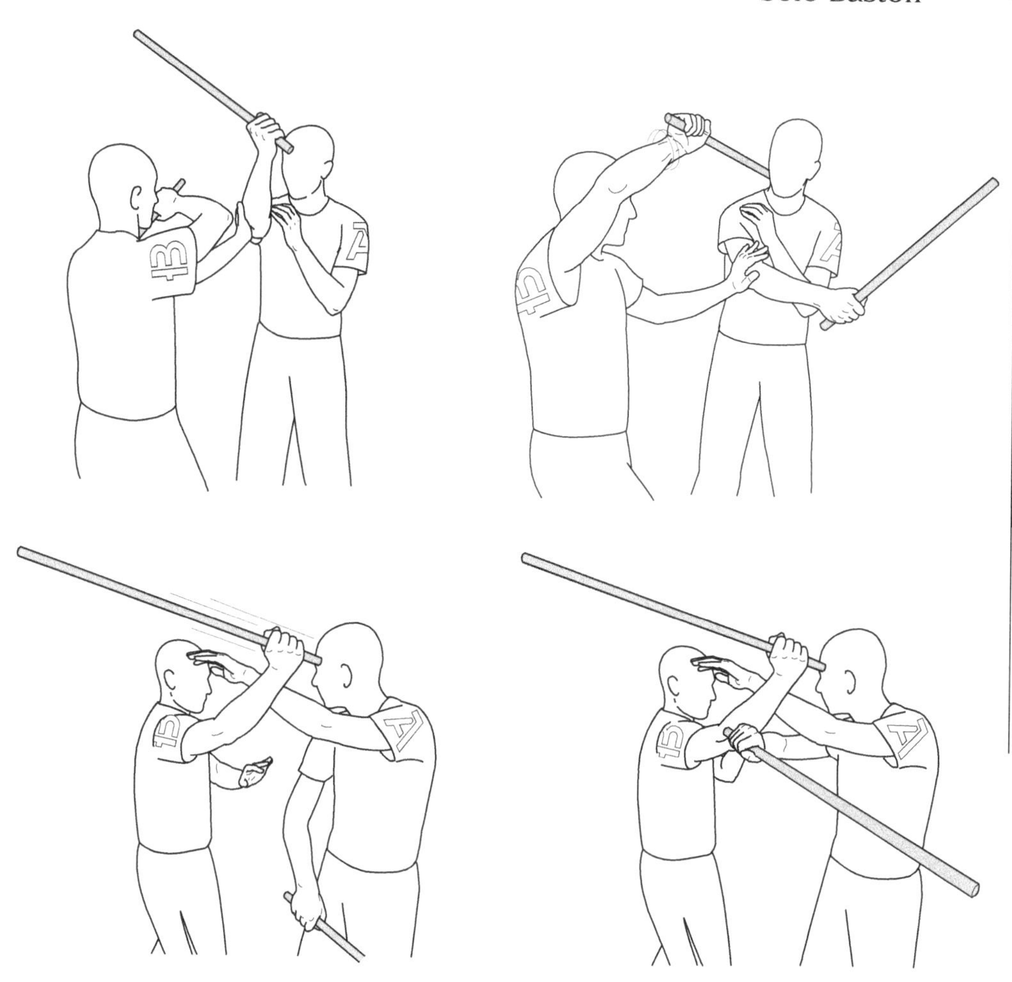

Another variation, can be to let the first attack pass instead of doing an interception:

1. A serves angle 1 Punyo strike
B uses a Retirada footwork — right leg stepping backward — while controlling the attack of A with his Check — putting his unarmed hand on the back of armed hand and following its movement.
2. B uses again Retirada to enter back in the range — right foot steps forward — and serves an angle 1 Punyo strike to the face
A counters with his unarmed arm at the level of the wrist...

Variations break the monotony of the drill and enrich it technically without bringing it to a stop.

Finalizations, as a disarm or a control with a takedown, do put an end to the drill.

SEQUENCE OF DRILLS

A very interesting exercise, that keeps the two partners focused, while offering changes of ranges and techniques, is to execute drills in sequence. When the two partners are accustomed to variety of drills, they can choose to associate some of them freely to form a longer and more complex pattern, a sort of 'super drill'.

EXAMPLE

Box Drill / Punyo Sumbrada / Box Drill / Hubud Lubud / Box Drill / Punyo Sumbrada…

That sequence of three drills has the advantage to train several ranges and to force the partners to stay in the present moment:

> A and B execute Box Drill (Medio Contrada range), and do several loops.
> It is A that first choose the moment of the transition to another drill, in this case Punyo Sumbrada.
> To this end, while it is his turn to serve an angle number 1, he will prepare a number 3 strike and gain some distance — using Retirada Caballero — to launch the Punyo Sumbrada drill.
> After several loops, it is time for B to choose the moment where he will step backward — while preparing a large number 1 — to come back to Box Drill.
> A and B take turn to ensure the transition between drills, with Box Drill as a central pattern of the exercise.

In the first instances, the transitions are marked — with a large movement of preparation of the strike — for the partner to easily identify the transition. Afterwards, that sign can be erased.

IV. DISARMS

If your opponent holds a weapon, you will significantly increase your chances of success in this combat by taking it from him. Many ways to disarm exist, and some schools do teach a plethora… and yet, present it as a technical richness inapplicable in real fight…

My own opinion on that matter… if you teach a disarm (and moreover any other technique) in a martial arts school, it must be applicable in a real situation, or be discarded.

To try to take the weapon or seize the hand of your opponent, to disarm him, while he tries hard to hurt you is actually a delicate move (if not dangerous). It must be trained again and again in order to be performed with flow, precision and engagement, and all that in a timely manner. This principle of opportunity is very important. A disarm, as a lock, does not work because we have decided so, but because at a moment of the fight we have the opportunity to do it (as the position of the opponent and our own allow it, for example). So, in order to be truly efficient, the training with a partner must be gradually re-evaluated to more realistic situations. The main concepts of the disarm must be 'physically' integrated. And maybe, only a handful of techniques of disarm, among the panel proposed, must be kept.

It is also important, as the stick stands for a long blade (machete, sword, etc…) in many exercises, to consider that specificity while doing the disarm. While facing a stick (broom handle, leg of a chair, expandable baton) we can seize it with our hand anywhere on its length without danger. Obviously, it is very different with a blade.

Before proceeding further, the two most simple disarms are to be mentioned. They are not spectacular, but they have proven their worth:
— a powerful strike to the armed hand of the opponent.
— a powerful strike to the head.

Now we will present you other techniques…
As for the teaching of the footworks, the disarm is first isolated to train it and understand its mechanics and principles. Of course, it will be later embedded in a more dynamic exercise in order to make it relevant and efficient.

Disarms Against Angle 1

Thumb Lock

Medio Contrada range
A serves an angle 1 strike
B counters, tip towards the ceiling, and checks
From the Check, B covers the fleshy part of the thumb of A, and thus can operate a thumb lock. Then he exerts a twist of the arm of A, until his little finger is towards the ceiling.

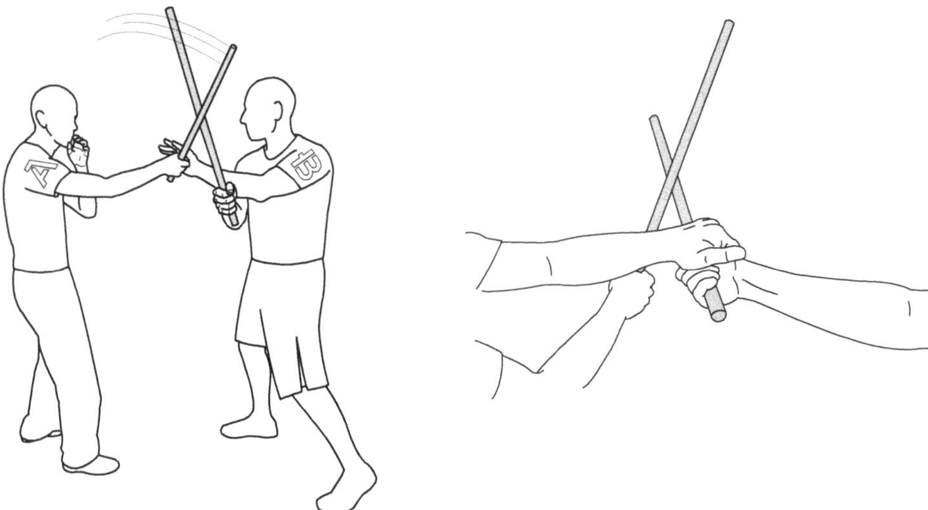

The subtlety of taking control of the fleshy part of the thumb is essential. Lower, to the wrist, A keeps a large part of the mobility of his hand, and that quickly turns into the advantage of the strongest. Higher, on the hand, B risks to cut himself if the weapon is sharp. And moreover, if he seizes the whole hand, he will close the fingers, and any disarm will be more difficult. The thumb is so his best asset to 'open the door' that will give him access to the weapon.

Once the control is ensured, the disarm is the result of two antagonist forces. Here: pull / push.

B, as if he intended to hit with his Punyo, comes into contact with the stick of A with his armed hand.
B pulls the hand of A in a direction and pushes the stick of A in another.

That push must be made as close as possible of the hand, always, and in such a way that the weapon tilts towards the opening of the fingers — and is not brought back into the palm. We exert then a sufficient pressure to release the weapon, while the hand is pulled.

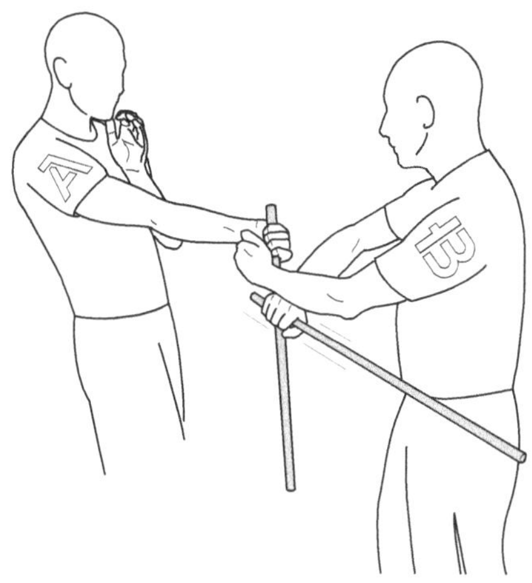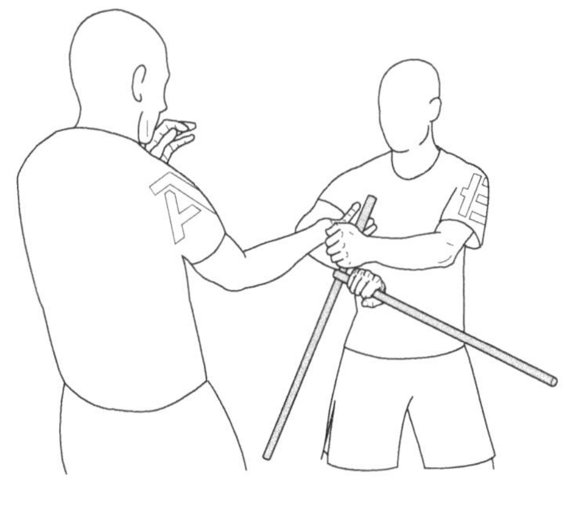

The success of the disarm depends on three factors (beside timing and opportunity in a real situation):

— opening of the prehension by taking control of the thumb.

— destructuration of A, by the twist of the arm (hand/wrist jonction -> elbow joint -> shoulder joint -> body structure).

— coordination of two antagonist forces: push on the weapon as close as possible of the hand to release it, and pull on the hand.

It is a disarm 'at a loss', as B disarms but does not appropriates the weapon of A.

Variation I: instead of releasing with the Punyo, we use a thrust to the abdomen to come into contact with the stick of A.

Variation II: still using the Punyo, but this time at the level of the Punyo of the weapon of A. It is the same disarm, but the release is made from above while threatening the head of A with the tip of the stick.

Scissors

Medio Contrada range
A serves an angle 1
B counters, tip towards the ceiling, and checks
B moves outside with a triangle footwork, while sliding his empty hand from his Check to the tip of the stick of A — it is important to keep control of the stick of the opponent, in order to free his own stick after the defense, and be able to strike back.
Simultaneously to his footwork, B strikes A to the elbow (funny bone) and lets his weapon follow its course until it rests on the forearm of A.
Then B disarms A with a shear stress. He moves up his armed hand and moves down his hand that holds the weapon of A. He applies antagonist forces.

At the end of that disarm, B has not only taken the weapon from A, but now holds a stick in each hand.

Disarms 'at a loss' are to be distinguished from those where the weapon of the opponent is grabbed and immediately available.

One of the keys of the success of this disarm is the triangle footwork. It allows to be ideally placed to use the arm of the opponent as a fulcrum to lever up.

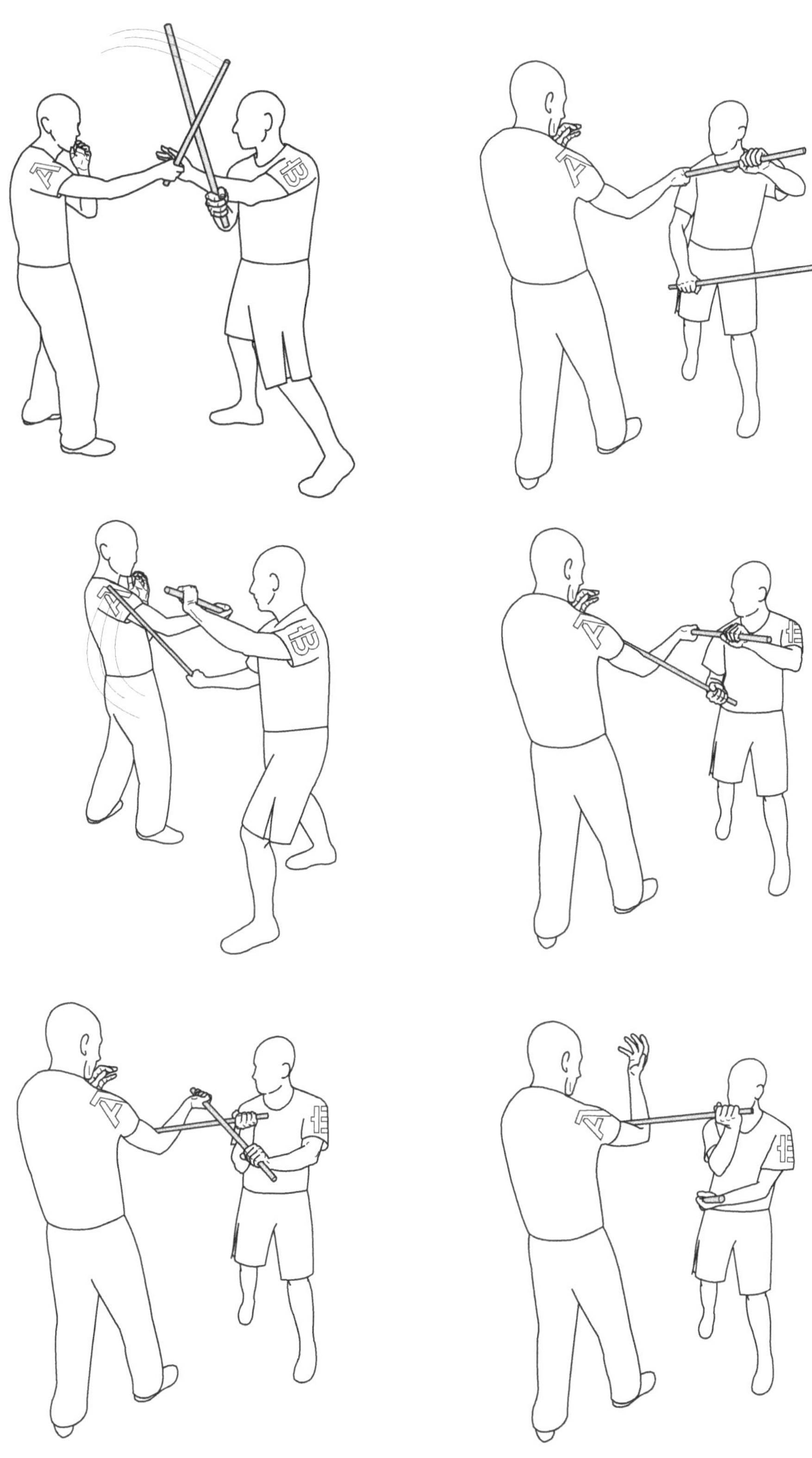

SNAKE

The Snake is a takeover of the arm of the opponent. To visualize that movement, think of your hand as the head of the snake, your forearm as its body, and the arm of your partner as a branch of a tree. The snake is going to wrap around the branch towards the trunk.

Medio Contrada range
A serves an angle 1
B counters, tip towards the ceiling, and checks
From his Check, B does a Snake
B serves an angle 4 Lobtik strike
B rams the armed forearm of A with his own, using Torque to support the movement. Normally, the tip of the stick of B hits simultaneously the head of A — while training, B will take care to control his attack, or that his partner uses proper protections

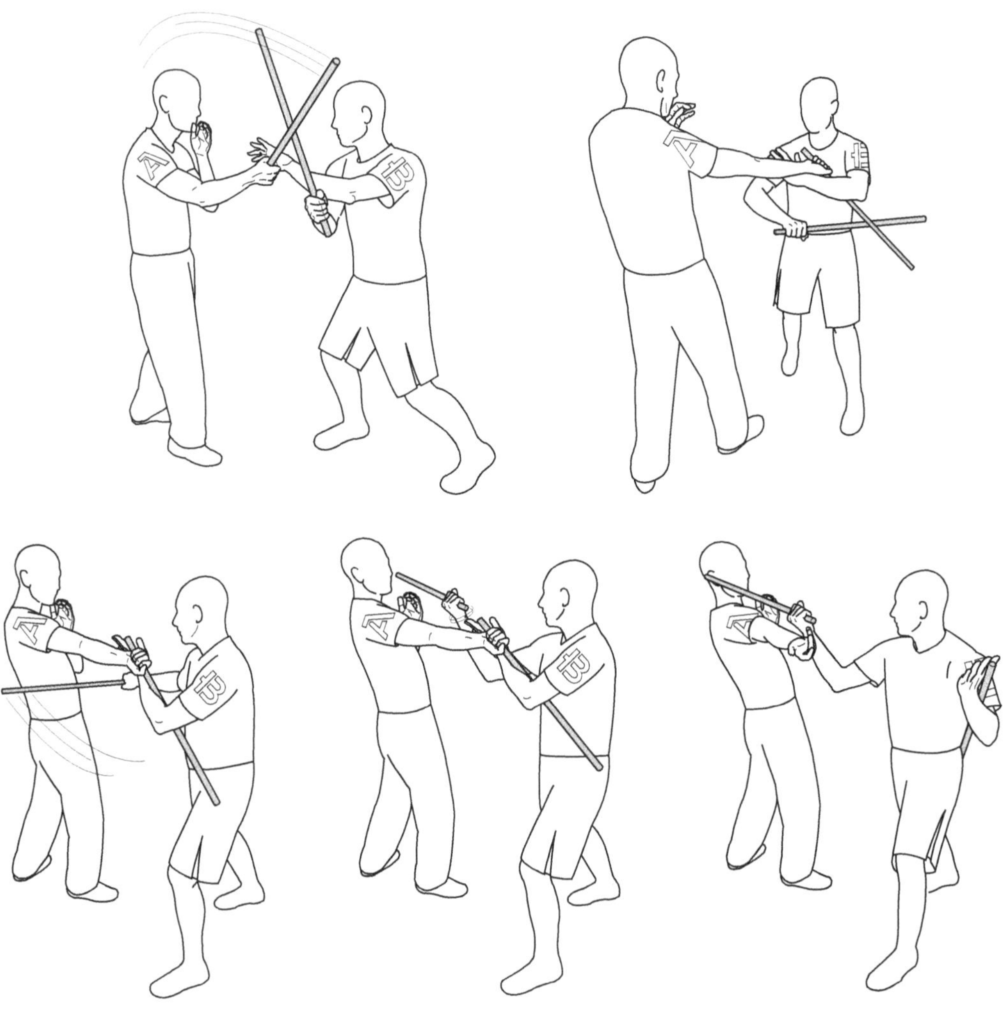

SNAKE 2

Medio Contrada range
A serves an angle 1
B counters, tip towards the ceiling, and checks
B makes a Snake with his stick: threat of thrust to the abdomen with the tip of his stick
B wraps by sticking his wrist to the wrist of A.
B amplifies his twist to release the stick

Variation: Once the Snake is locked, B throws a direct punch to the face with his unarmed hand. When his arm comes back, he seizes his own stick and pulls it backward, thus causing the disarm. (It is an option, if the first version of the disarm is stuck.)

DISARM 5

Medio Contrada range
A serves an angle 1
B counters, tip towards the floor, and checks
B seizes the stick of A as closely as possible to the hand, while making a twist to bring the little finger towards the ceiling
Simultaneously B hits the face of A with his Punyo
B does a few strikes in order to place his stick below
B pulls down the stick of A and moves up his own to hit the wrist of A and fetch the weapon

It is interesting to hit some strikes while moving your stick in the adequate position for the disarm. It is even fundamental in a real situation, where the opportunity to remove his weapon from your opponent will be determined by preliminary strikes.

When A is hit in the face, or 'busy' with the threat of a strike (like in previous disarms), he is a lot less able to resist to the twist of his arm, or the seizure of his stick.

DISARM 6

This disarm is quite alike the previous one, except for the finalization.

Medio Contrada range
A serves an angle 1
B counters, tip towards the floor, and checks
B seizes the stick of A as closely as possible of the hand
B hits simultaneously with several strikes to place his stick below.
B brings the little finger of A towards the ceiling with a twist
B, with an upward move, catch on the wrist of A with his Punyo
B pushes with an upward swing of his elbow (as if he was doing a downward punch), while he pulls on the stick of A, using the principle of antagonist forces

Disarm 5

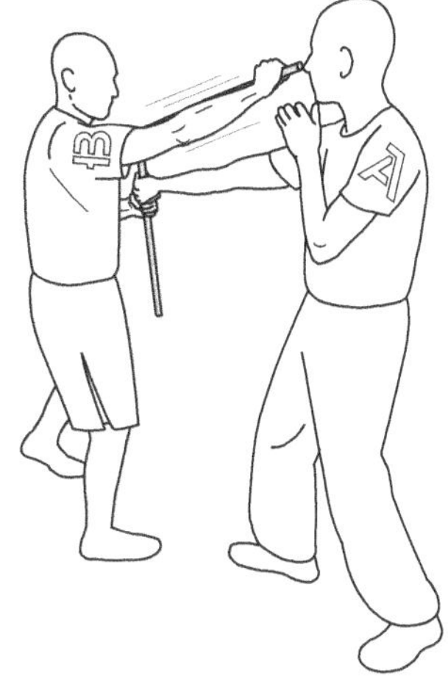

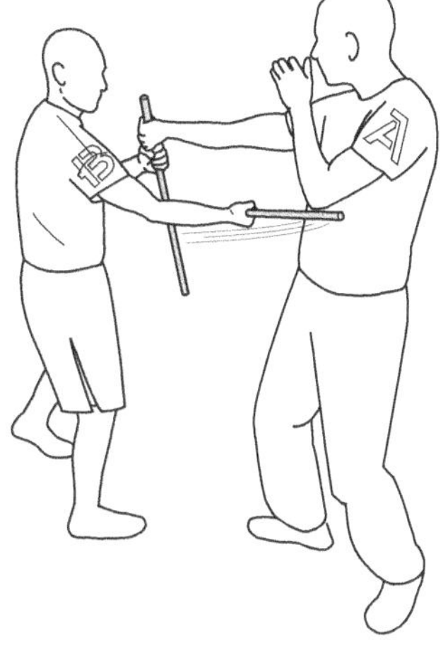

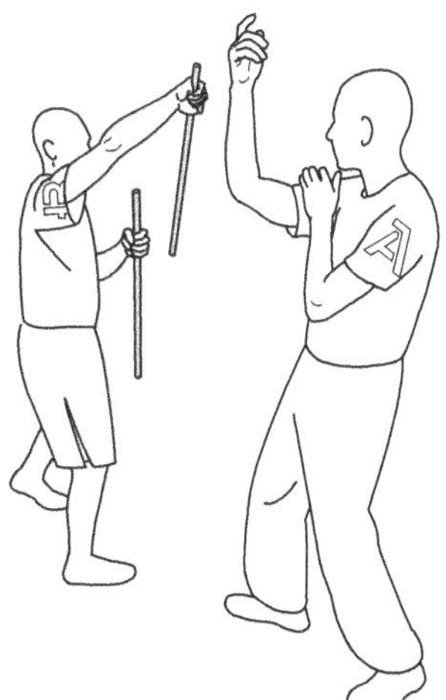

DISARM 7

Medio Contrada range
A serves an angle 1
B counters, tip towards the floor, and checks
B seizes the stick of A as closely as possible to the hand, and twists to bring the little finger of A towards the ceiling
B pulls on the stick of A while he hits the wrist of A from above with his armed hand — ideally, this blow is a vertical Abaniko threatening the head

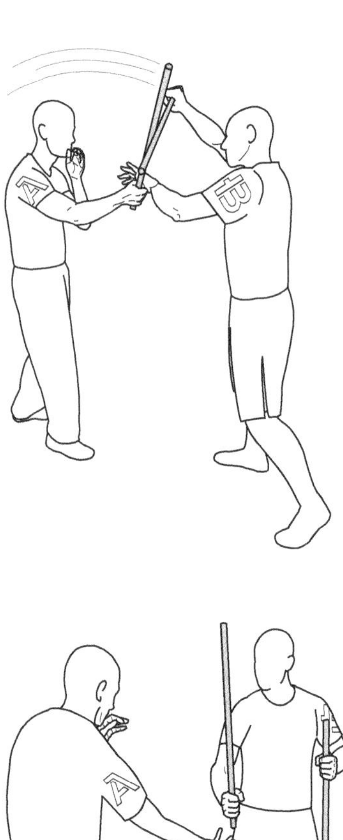

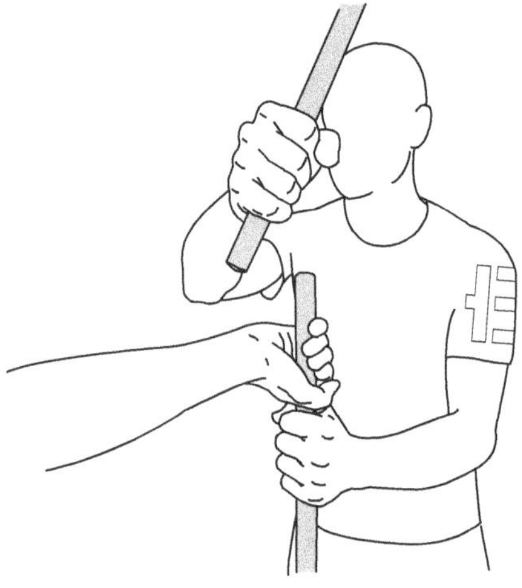

DISARMS AGAINST ANGLE 2

THUMB LOCK

Medio Contrada range
A serves an angle 2
B counters and checks
B serves a thrust to the throat and, from the Check, seizes the fleshy part of the thumb of A
B places his armed wrist against the stick of A as closely as possible to the hand
B releases the stick by pulling on the hand of A while pushing on the stick with his wrist

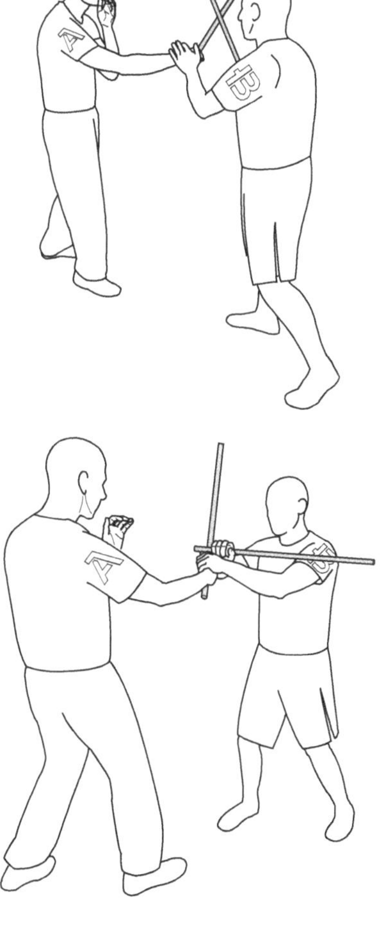

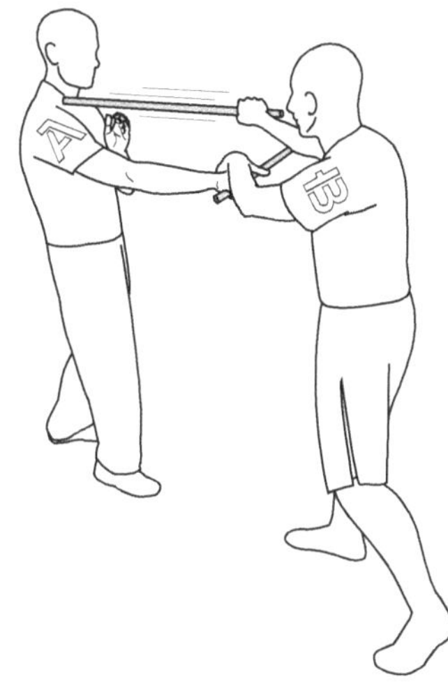

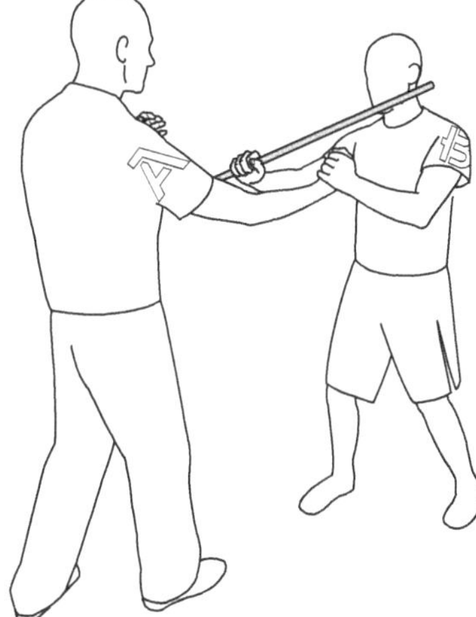

REVERSED SNAKE

Medio Contrada range
A serves an angle 2
B counters and checks
B initiates a thrust threatening the abdomen and follows his move to do a Snake with his armed hand
B releases the stick of A with his unarmed hand

Variation I: as soon as he controls the arm of A with his Snake, B pivots on the outside. He then rams the arm of A with his unarmed forearm, just above the elbow. With the violent effect of the arm lock, A drops his weapon. While training, we push on the elbow joint with our palm (rather then ramming with the forearm), in order to preserve our partner.

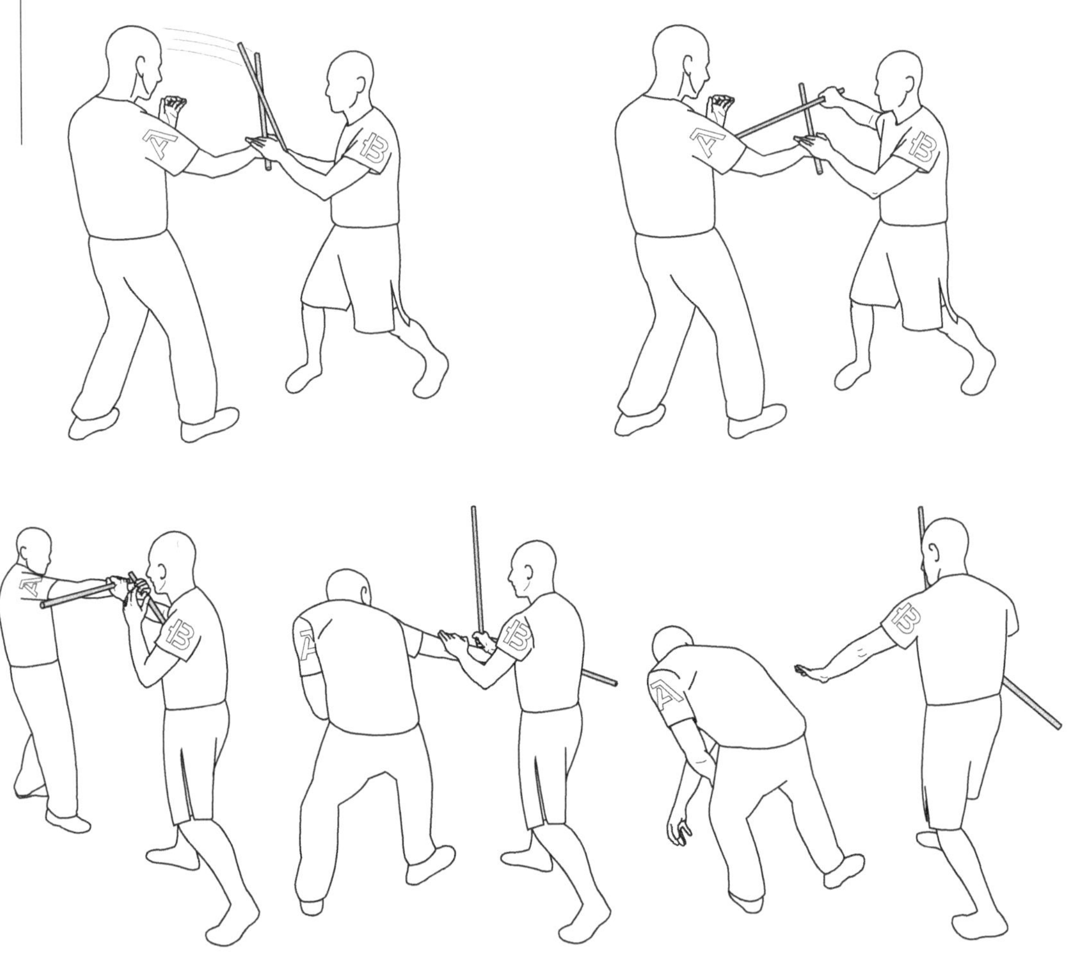

SNAKE

Medio Contrada range
A serves an angle 2
B counters and checks
B takes control of the arm of A with a Snake with his unarmed hand (stay at the level of the wrist in order to not lock the arm)
B comes from above with his Punyo to make a shearing move
The Snake pushes to one side, the angle wrist / Punyo pushes to the other side
A is disarmed

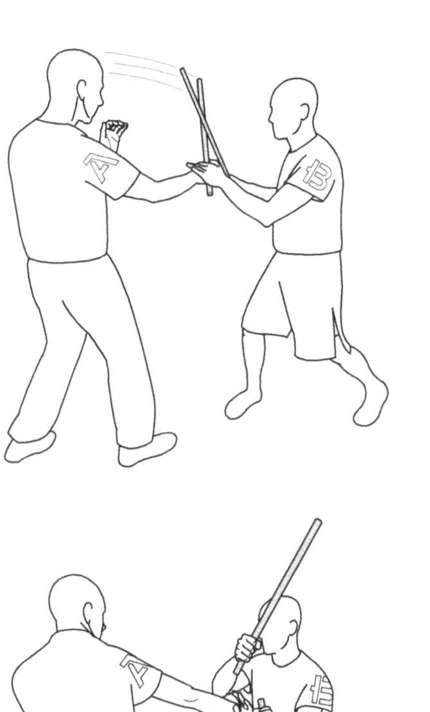

DISARMS AGAINST ANGLE 5

DISARM 1

Medio Contrada range
A serves a thrust angle 5
B counters, tip towards the ceiling, and checks
B catches the wrist of A and slips his stick in the space between his own arm and the stick of A to come thumb against thumb
With a sudden twist of the wrist, B releases the stick of A

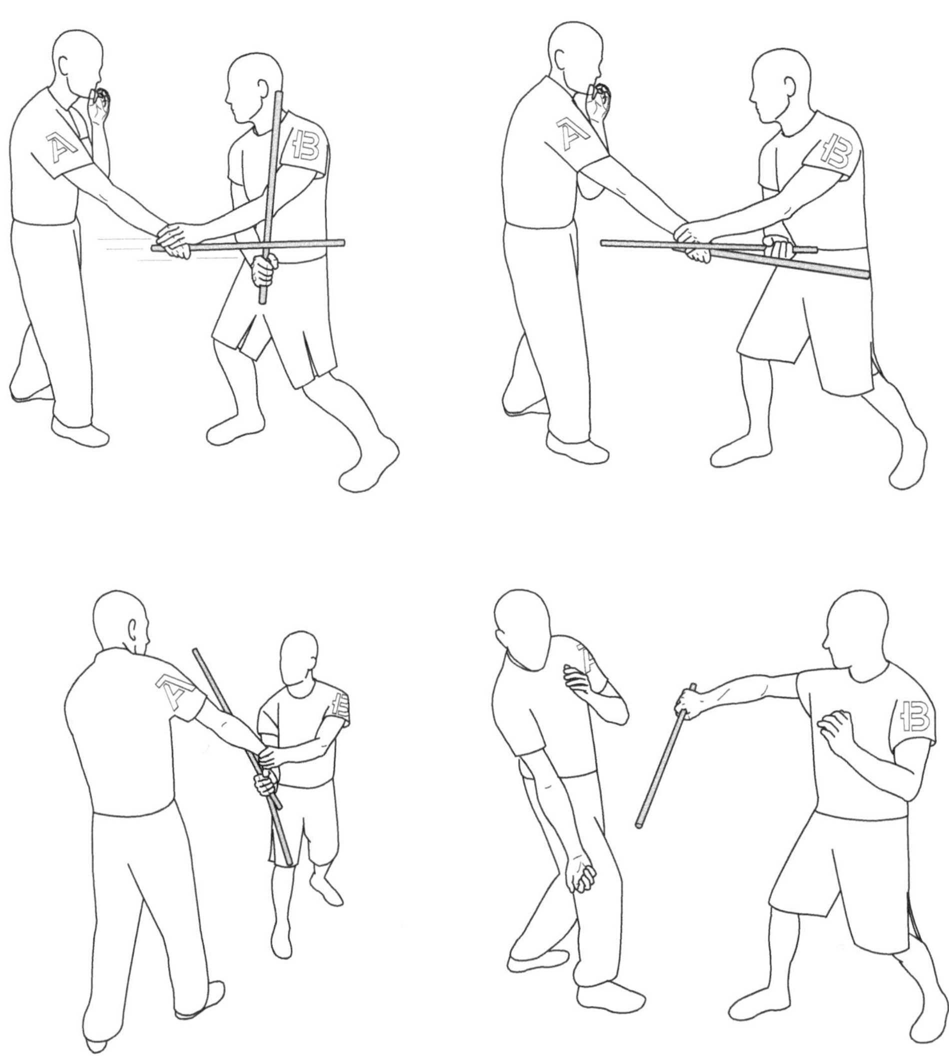

DISARM 2

Medio Contrada range
A serves a thrust angle 5
B counters, tip towards the floor, and checks
From his Check, B seizes the stick of A
B pulls on the stick while ramming the hand of A from above — while training, using his wrist… if not, with his Punyo

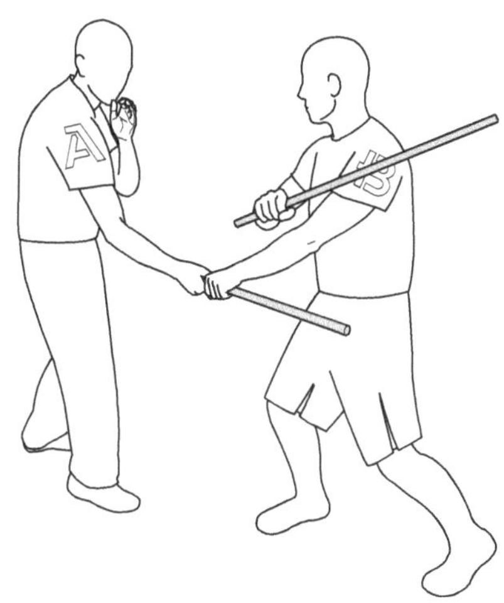

V. Applications

The applications, or confrontations, are exercises for two partners, sometimes more, rather classical in most martial arts. An eskrimador does a particular attack, or a particular sequence, and his partner must react, following a specified number of guidelines given by the teacher. So, several elements can be implemented in one exercise: concept of range, timing, footwork, quality of the counter, opportunity and precision of the counterattacks, disarm and/or takedown. And although it can be done with intensity and determination, it is still not sparring or fight. The partners are in the 'comfortable' and secured context of an exercise of which the parameters are known. Thus, they can focus on the quality of the technique, and sometimes rather complex sequences.

For the examples of applications that follow, the partners A and B are both armed with a stick held in the right hand. Nonetheless, It is also recommended to train the left hand, with the necessary adaptations, if only to take account of the left-handed students.

Counter and Counterattacks Medio Contrada Range

A and B are facing each other at a range where they can both reach numerous targets. To counter with a block is relevant and a Check can also be done.

It is a tighten range of training where we could be tempted to move away (with a Retirada for example) to have more space. But it is precisely asked to the eskrimador to train De Fondo, to remain where he is — to develop his technical ease in spite of the shortening of the movements, but also to keep all the options of available counterattacks.

There are two types of reactions: the immediate reactions, varieties of counterattacks (strike to the hand, strike to the head, thrust...) that follow directly the defense and can alone put an end to the confrontation by incapacitating the opponent; the complementary reactions that enrich the options (disarm, redirect the arm, lock,...) without being essential.

IMMEDIATE REACTION 1: COUNTERATTACK ON THE HAND

Medio Contrada range, A and B are facing
each other in guard position
A serves an angle 1 strike
B counters and checks
B use his Check to get some space by push-
ing away the armed hand of A
B serves a strike to the hand of A

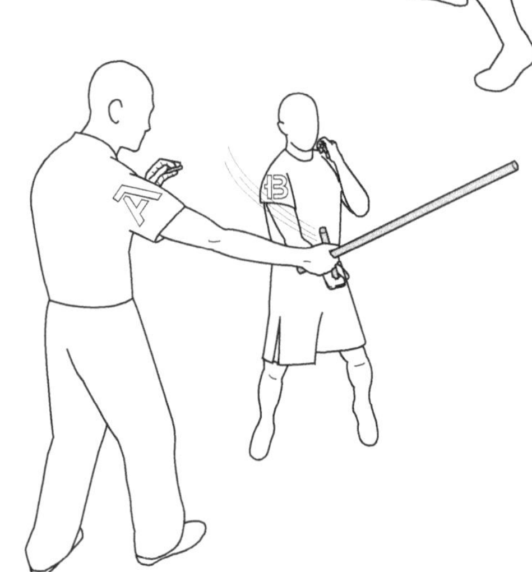

The same exercise is done using the first 5
angles of attack — on the principle of 'your turn /
my turn'.

IMMEDIATE REACTION 2: COUNTERATTACK TO THE HEAD

Same exercise, but B counterattacks with
a strike to the head of A, potentially using
his Check — push, do not grab — to move
the weapon of A out of the way.

Here again, and for all the following
exercises, it is done using the first 5 angles
of attack — on the principle of 'your turn /
my turn'.

IMMEDIATE REACTION 3: MULTIPLE COUNTERATTACKS TO THE BODY

Same exercise, but B makes multiple counterattacks (3 to 5 strikes) to the body, trying to vary the targets and the levels. He will also try to link his strikes in a fluid and logical sequence. For example:

Medio Contrada range
A serves angle 2
B counters and checks
B strikes angle 3 to the abdomen, angle 2 to the thigh and angle 1 to the shoulder

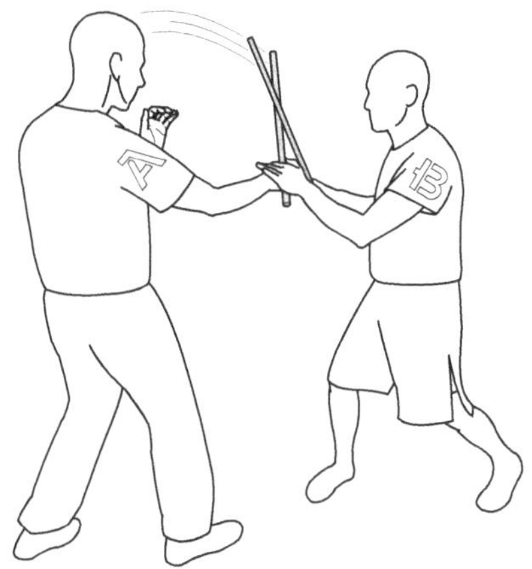

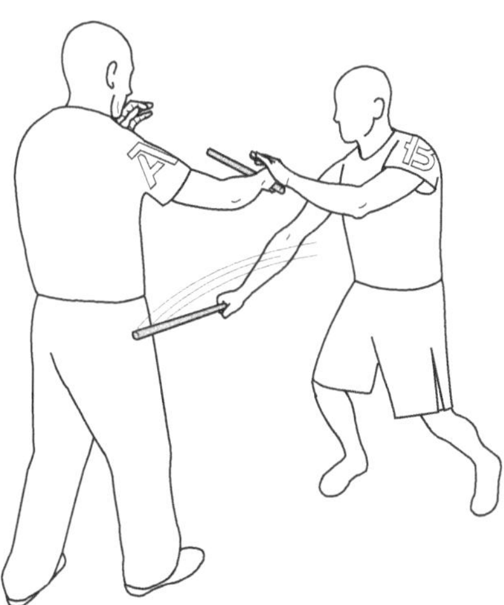

IMMEDIATE REACTION 4: COUNTERATTACK WITH THE PUNYO

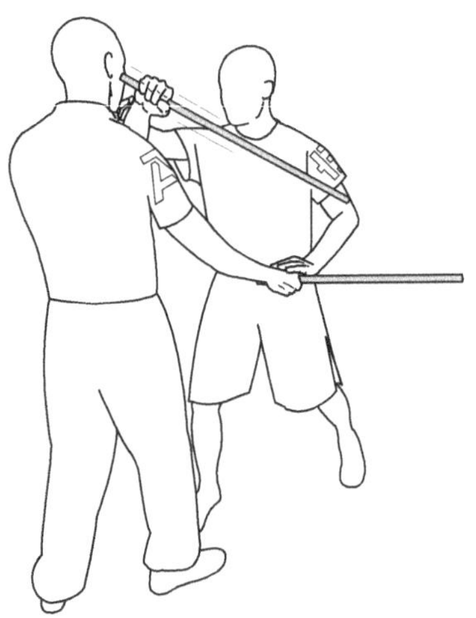

Same exercise, but B hits with his Punyo. If he strikes the hand, he can stay where he is. But to hit the body or the head, he must come closer with a footwork (step or half-step).

For the training, on a principle 'your turn / my turn', if B has stepped in with a half-step, he steps out with a half-step, before it is his turn to serve. If he has stepped in with a step, he steps out with a step. Thus, the ability to get in and the ability to get out are trained.

IMMEDIATE REACTION 5: COUNTERATTACK WITH A NATURAL WEAPON

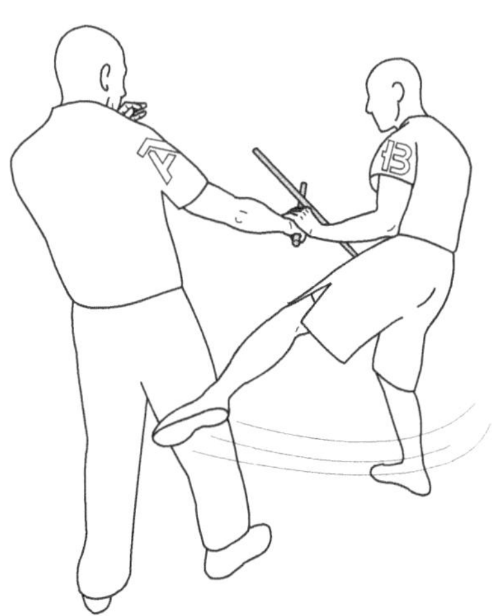

This time, the counterattack is done with the unarmed hand or a leg. As for the Punyo, if a footwork is necessary to get closer, it is done. But the same footwork (step or half-step) is done to get back in the initial range.

IMMEDIATE REACTION 6: COUNTER-ATTACK WITH ABANIKO

Same exercise, but B hits with an Abaniko. To the hand, to the head or at the body, but an Abaniko strike.

IMMEDIATE REACTION 7: COUNTERATTACK WITH A THRUST

A reminder of the use of a long blade, B counterattacks this time with a thrust. Although it may seem less relevant with a stick, this training with the thrust is kept, whatever the area targeted.

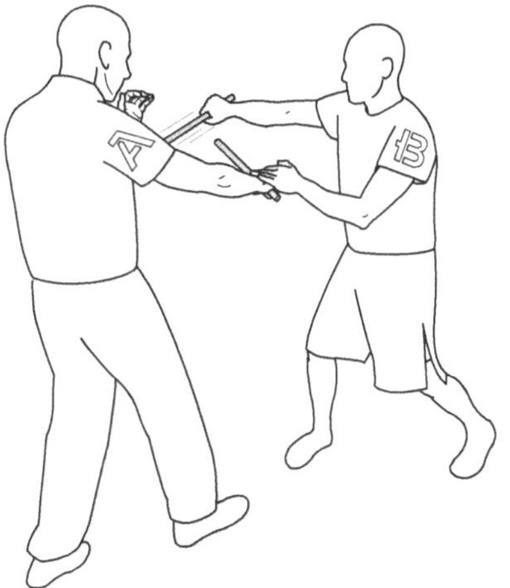

IMMEDIATE REACTION 8: COUNTERATTACK WITH DOS MANOS

Same exercise, but B grabs his stick with his two hands to ram the target. Here again, it may be necessary to get closer with a footwork, and to train the step back with the same footwork, as seen while training the counterattack with the Punyo.

MIX THE IMMEDIATE REACTIONS

So, we have eight variations of the Immediate Reactions. In order to make them more functional, the eskrimadors are invited — always in an exercise 'your turn / my turn' in response to an attack on the angles 1 to 5 — to mix two, three or four of these options. For example:

    A serves an angle 3 strike
    B counters and checks
    B pushes the hand of A and strikes it with his stick
    B follows with three strikes to the body
    B grabs his stick with his two hands and, with a half-step, rams the throat of A
    B gets back in the initial range with a half-step

The goal is to produce logical and coherent sequences, but still being creative. On the other hand, multiplying the footworks and getting in and out of the range several times, for example, is to be avoided.

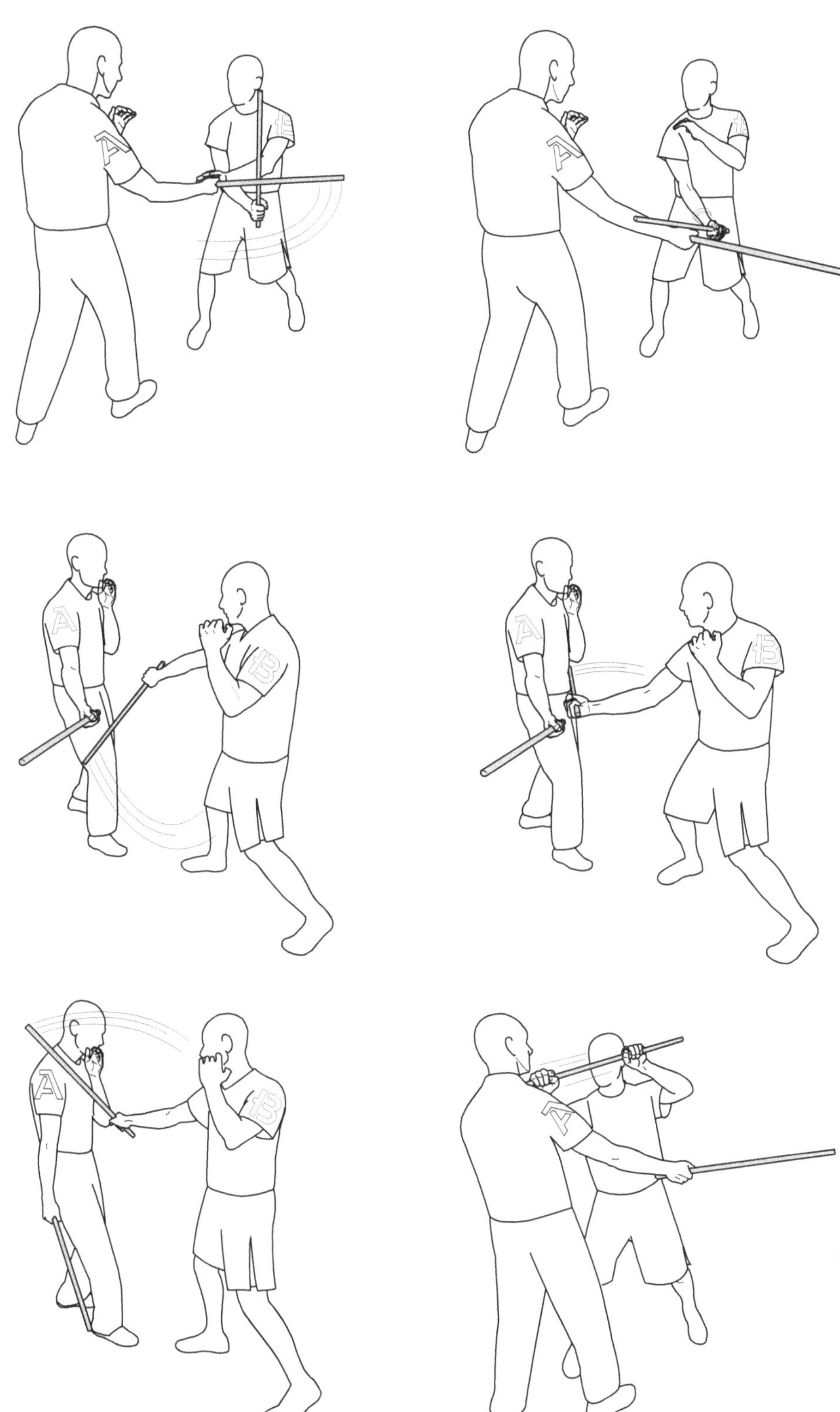

Applications Medio Range

COMPLEMENTARY REACTIONS

In a well-planned counterattack , a complementary reaction follows one, two or three immediate reactions. To do an immediate reaction is essential... the complementary reaction is an option.

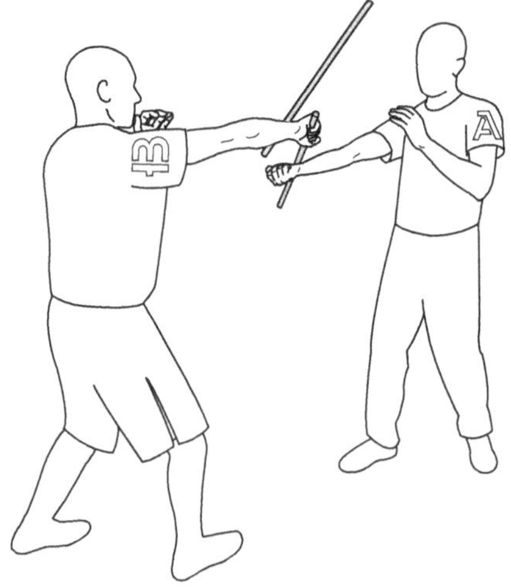

In the first of the training, the complementary reaction is isolated, but keep in mind the fundamental previous rule.

For the exercise, A and B are facing each other in guard position, at Medio Contrada range. A serves angle 1, B counters and does the complementary reaction. B serves angle 1, A does the complementary reaction. A serves 2... 'your turn / my turn' from angle 1 to 5.

1. Disarm

2. Redirection

After he has countered the attack of A, B makes contact with the arm of A, with his armed forearm or his unarmed hand. He then redirects it to create new options — or possibly to close options of A.

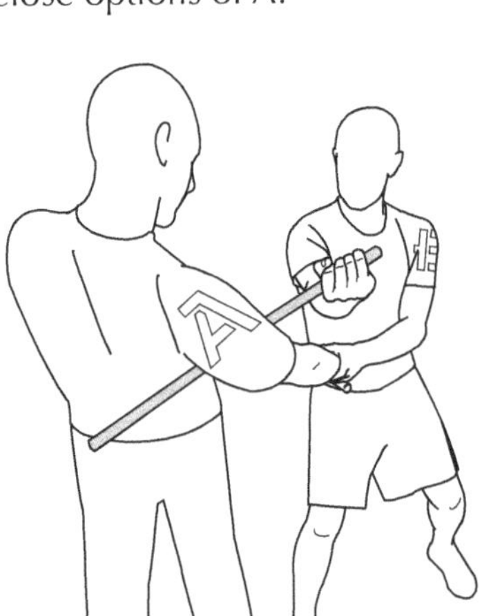

3. Joint Constraint

In an context of armed combat, a joint constraint is used to manipulate the opponent, notably in order to make him present targets that he can't protect.

Mix Immediate Reactions and Complementaries Reactions

Now we have enough training material and knowledge to get to another level and mix immediate reactions and complementary reactions.

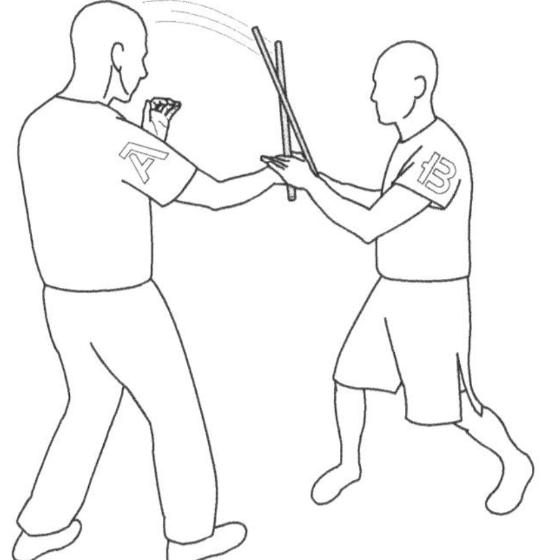

Dynamic training with a partner allows to develop a technical quality of which some elements will be available in a degraded situation of a real fight. Of course, the numbers and the coherence of these elements depend of the time and the application invested in the training, and thus of the repetitions.

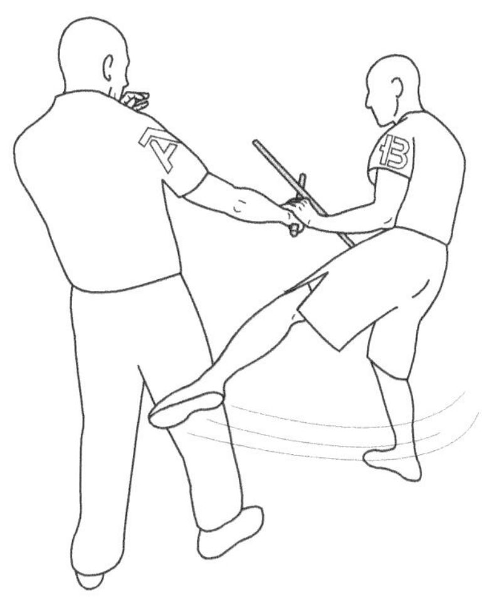

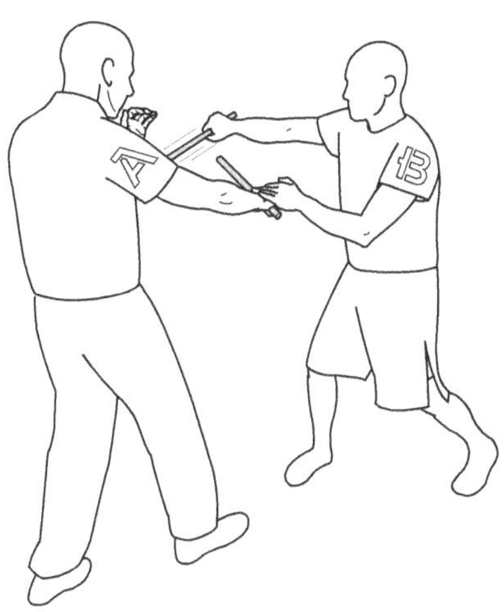

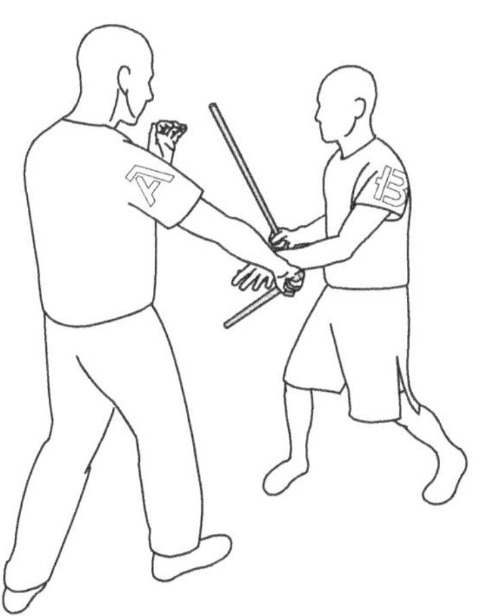

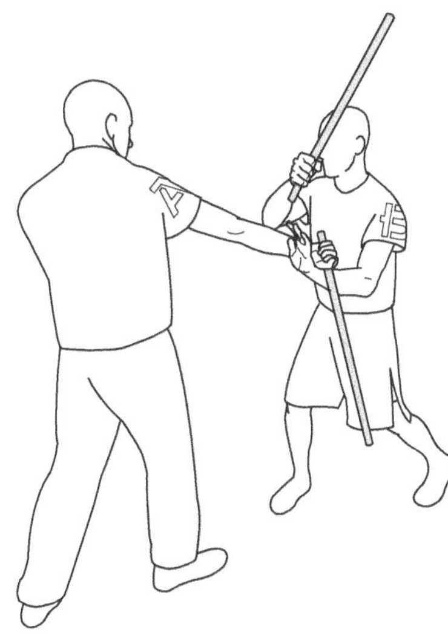

COUNTER AND COUNTERATTACKS LARGO MANO RANGE

When we undergo an assault, it is not opportune to stay where the opponent hopes we will be, as he applies all the power of his attack on that impact point. And it will be difficult to develop a counter sufficient to stop it, at the risk of being hit or losing structure, and being unable to react to the following strikes. So, we will use footworks and body mobility to deal with the attack.

TRIANGLE

Largo Mano range, A and B are facing each other in guard position
A steps forward using an half-step, in order to strike B to the body with a large angle 1 Lobtik attack
B steps out of the axis with a triangle footwork while doing a defense with the tip of his stick towards the floor and a Check (the two partners are now at Medio Contrada range)
B follows immediately with a strike to the armed hand of A

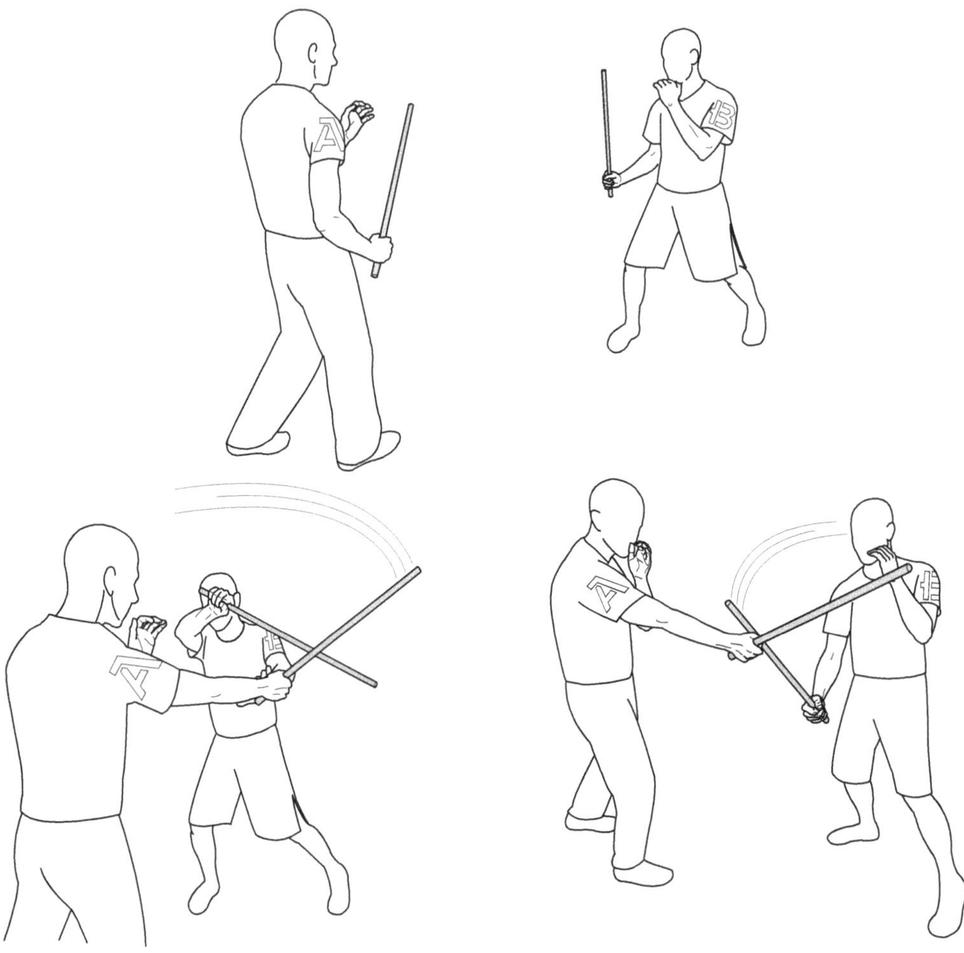

Variation 1:
B counterattacks with a strike to the body.

Variation 2:
B counterattacks with a strike to the head.

Variation 3:
B does three counterattacks in sequence, varying targets and levels, thrusts and cuts.

It is important to note that B is not static after his first step. He will move to maintain optimal range in order to strike with the last four inches of his weapon — or, at the contrary, to reduce the range in order to strike with the Punyo.

In a self-defense concept, where preserving ourselves and searching for 'exit doors' is crucial, B will use his footworks to move past A while doing his strikes.

It is interesting to do Checks with the unarmed hand. That allows to train blows with that hand — just because we have a weapon doesn't leave us one-armed ! It is also a good mean to check the range and the position of the body of the opponent, which may have made an evade technique, or be laying on the floor after a strike.

Obviously, that exercise must be trained with attacks in the other angles. On angle 1 and 3, the initial triangle footwork is inside. On angle 2 and 4, it is an outside triangle footwork. On an angle 5 thrust, we will favor a step aside, inside or outside.

The choice to counter with the tip towards the ceiling or the tip towards the floor will induce a variation of the counterattack immediately available. The important concept is to follow with the most direct strike, the most natural from the position where the weapon stands, without any need to cock it. The quickness and the flow of the eskrimador come with the relaxed training and the elimination of the unnecessary gestures and amplitudes.

PIVOT

In the previous training, we choose deliberately to reduce the distance or, more simply, to move forward on the attack.

Here, we will step out of the range of the weapon with a backward footwork. In order to do so, Retirada Caballero (half-step), Retirada Ilustrisimo (step), or the pivot can be used.

Largo Mano range
A steps forward on B with a large angle 1 strike
B does a pivot to get out of the attack
Simultaneously he leaves his stick on the trajectory of the hand of A

The most important is to do, in the right timing, the defensive footwork. That doesn't keep from leaving a little 'gift' on the way. The more A hits hard, the more his inertia is great, the more he has chances to disarm himself when his hand encounters the stick of B. In the idea of a fight with long blades, it is the edge of the weapon that is turned towards the trajectory of the armed hand of A.

Largo Mano range
A steps forward on B with a large angle 1 strike
B does a pivot to get out of the attack
Simultaneously he leaves his stick on the trajectory of the hand of A
B comes back in the range (unfold his pivot) with a thrust to the throat
B strikes the leg with an angle 6 Lobtik
B finalizes with an angle 1 strike to the head

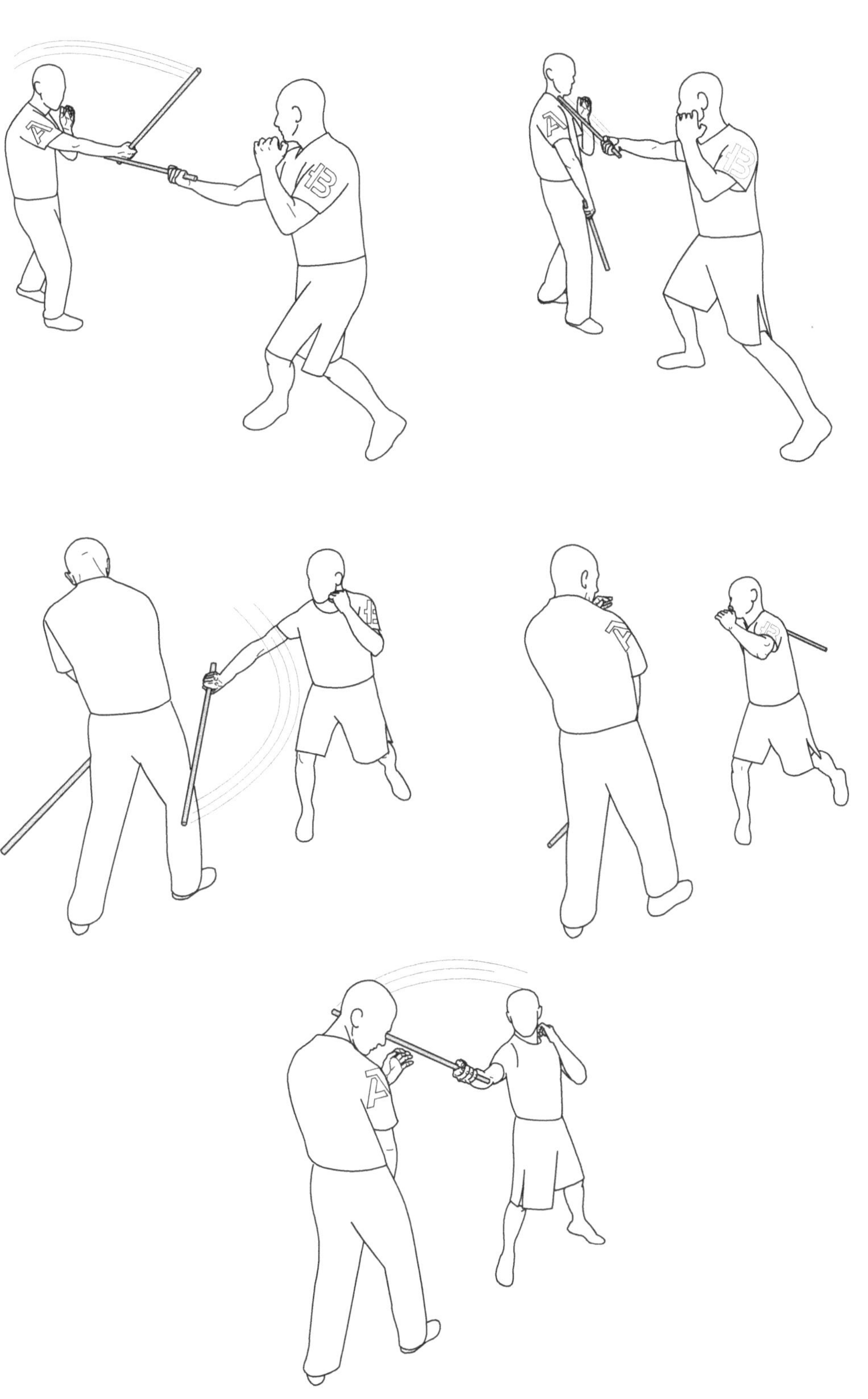

ELASTIKO

This time, we exaggerate our body mechanics in a defensive move to get out of the range of the attack.

Largo Mano range
A steps forward on B with a large angle 1 strike
B dodges with his chest while staying where he stands
Simultaneously he makes contact with the armed wrist of A with his own stick, using a crossed strike (it forms an X with the attack of A)

If, while dodging with a pivot, we could afford to miss the hand of A, here it is imperative to hit — or we will be totally exposed to the following attack. For safety, an immediate second strike to the hand will be executed.

Largo Mano range
B dodges with his chest while staying where he stands
Simultaneously he makes contact with the armed wrist of A with his own stick, using a crossed strike
B follows with a redondo strike to the hand, before A comes back.
B does a triangle footwork on the outside and strikes angle 2 Lobtik to the head
B strikes angle 7 Lobtik to the leg
B finalizes with an angle 2 Lobtik strike to the head, while putting back distance between A and him, pivoting with a step aside, and ends in Abierta guard position

TRIANGLE TOWARDS THE ATTACK

Here we use triangle footwork and body mobility. The purpose is to dodge the strike to the body while offering a counterattack at the wrist, or the forearm, on which impacts (with a stick) are similar to cuts (with a long blade).

Largo Mano range
A steps in with a half-step and serves a large angle 1 Lobtik
B does an outside triangle footwork while dodging the strike of A by lowering his torso (in fact, by lowering his stands). He moves under the attack of A.
Meanwhile, he lets his weapon drift on the trajectory of the arm of A. We can easily imagine the application with a long blade.
B follows with an angle 2 Lobtik strike to the knee
B regains some distance while serving a redondo to the shoulder or to the head

Against a number 2 attack, same principle:

Largo Mano range
A steps in with a step and serves a large angle 2 Lobtik
B does an inside triangle footwork while moving under the attack of A
Meanwhile, he lets his weapon on the trajectory of the arm of A
B regains some distance while serving an angle 1 strike to the head

The triangle footwork followed by the regain of distance, with a pivot on the front foot, corresponds to the female triangle and step aside described in the previous chapter.

Always with the idea of stepping while hitting the armed arm of the partner in the movement of his attack, we will train on angles from 1 to 5. The priority is the sidestep, the counterattack to the arm is secondary.

Largo Mano range
A serves angle 1 Lobtik reducing the distance
B does outside triangle and dodges while hitting the arm of A
A goes back to Largo range
A serves angle 2 Lobtik while moving forward
B does inside triangle and dodges while hitting the arm of A
A goes back to Largo Mano range
A serves angle 3 Lobtik while moving forward
B does Retirada Ilustrisimo while exaggerating his body mechanics (Elastiko) to hit the arm of A from above
A goes back to Largo range
A serves angle 4 Lobtik while moving forward
B goes out and does a crossed strike from above to the arm of A
A goes back to Largo range
A serves an angle 5 thrust while moving forward
B has the choice to move out with an inside triangle or an outside triangle...

When A has served the 5 angles, A and B exchange their roles and B serves the angles 1 to 5 while A dodges and counterattacks.
A variation is to train the exercise in a 'your turn / my turn' principle.

DYNAMIC APPLICATION: 1 / 2 / 1

To train our applications, an initial little drill is used as a basis to have a more dynamic exercise than the previous ones, where we started directly from the attack.

TRIANGLE

Largo Mano range, A and B are facing each other in guard position
A and B do in sequence angle 1 Lobtik and angle 2 Lobtik
On the third movement, an angle 1 Lobtik strike, A reduces the distance with a half-step
B goes out of the axis with a triangle footwork and counters

A fine timing is imperative. If B waits for A to deploy is attack to counter, his defense will be ineffective. He must identify the moment where A initiates his attack to move. Too early, A will have a chance to change the angle. Too late, the inertia of the strike will not be absorbed.

We can first train this timing with repetitions of the previous exercise on a principle 'your turn / my turn':

Largo Mano range, A and B are facing each other in guard position
A and B do in sequence angle 1 Lobtik and angle 2 Lobtik
On the third movement, an angle 1 Lobtik strike, A reduces the distance with a half-step
B goes out of the axis with a triangle footwork and counters
A goes back to Largo range with a backward half-step
A and B do in sequence angle 1 Lobtik and angle 2 Lobtik
On the third movement, B does a half-step and serves angle 1
A does a triangle footwork and counters
B goes back to Largo…

Once the timing acquired, sequences can be trained.

Largo Mano range, A and B are facing each other in guard position
A and B do in sequence angle 1 Lobtik and angle 2 Lobtik
A does a half-step and serves angle 1 Lobtik
B does a triangle footwork and counters, tip towards the ceiling, and checks
B strikes to the leg angle 6 Lobtik
B follows with angle 3 Lobtik and angle 4, leaving his stick in contact with the ribs of A
B finalizes with a lock, using his stick diagonally against the biceps and the back of A, and his control on the wrist of A with his unarmed hand
B pivots to drag A to the ground

That exercise is particularly ideal to train the disarms in a dynamic context, possibly with some previous strikes:

Largo Mano range
A and B do in sequence angle 1 Lobtik and angle 2 Lobtik
When A steps in and serves angle 1, B does a triangle footwork and counters, tip towards the floor, and checks
B does three strikes to the body in sequence (1/4/3), while keeping his control on the armed hand of A with his Check
B seizes the stick of A as closely as possible to the hand, and twists to bring the little finger towards the ceiling, while doing an outside triangle footwork
B brings down the stick of A and brings up his own to pull off and retrieve the weapon
B regains some distance to take advantage of being now armed with two sticks while his opponent has only his bare hands.

To train against attacks on angle 2, the partner enters on the second movement with a step instead of waiting for the third to reduce the distance.

Largo Mano range
A and B serve angle 1 Lobtik
A does a step and serves angle 2 Lobtik
B goes out with an outside triangle footwork, counters and checks
B strikes A to the head while doing a thumb lock from his Check
B releases the stick of A by bringing back his own stick, as closely as possible to the hand
B regains some distance while delivering some strikes to dissuade A from following him.

PIVOT

Largo Mano range
A and B do in sequence angle 1 Lobtik and angle 2 Lobtik
A does a half-step and serves an angle 1 Lobtik
B dodges with a pivot while doing a crossed strike, ideally on the hand of A
B goes back in the range and strikes to the thigh with an angle 6 Lobtik
B follows with a redondo on the arm, or the shoulder, and angle 2 Lobtik to the head
B finalizes with a low kick
B regains some distance with a half-step

BABY SPARRING

As the name suggests, it is a preparatory exercise for the sparring, on a principle 'your turn / my turn'. According to the trust between the two partners, and the degree of intensity they wish to engage, they can train with foam sticks, or wear protections (helmets, gloves, forearms guards, chest guard,…). In a first phase, it is advisable to train with controlled intensity, without protections, to focus on the technical quality.

Largo Mano range, A and B are facing each other
A engages an open attack
B chooses to counter or to dodge
B serves an open attack
A counters or dodges
A serves an open attack
B counters or…

The two partners must be very mobile, able to change rhythm and erase the superfluous movements.

SPARRING

The sparring, necessary to put our technical quality and our combativeness to the test, must be done under the supervision of an instructor. There are several levels of sparring, and teacher and partners determine together which one is appropriate:

— sticks wrapped in foam and full protections
— foam sticks, without protections
— rattan sticks (light and thin sticks) and full protections
— rattan sticks and light protections (groin guard, gloves and helmet)
— rattan sticks without protections
— possibility to also engage attacks with legs and fist
— one opponent against several
— three against three
— ...

My personal predilection goes to exchanges with rattan sticks and light protections. Exchanges with foam sticks often become muddled, and the partners quickly neglect the hits received, losing realism about their own protection.

The rattan stick for competition, lighter and thinner than the one used in training, leaves on the forearms, the thighs or the flank nice bruises that 'sting', without the risk of a fracture or an actual injury. The impacts on the gloves and the helmet offer dull sounds unequivocal — you have been hit. In this configuration, the eskrimador is sufficiently worried about the contact with the stick of his opponent to develop a defensive strategy, while keeping a good part of game and adrenaline.

CARENZA

The Carenza corresponds to the shadow training of the boxing. That exercise, deservedly very valued, consists in training techniques in thin air with footwork, facing an imaginary opponent. The shadow is the best way for the eskrimador as it is the expression of his body ease and his understanding of the art.

Doble Baston

A stick in each hand, the eskrimador is ready for the art of combat with two weapons: Doble Baston or Sinawali (Filipino word, that means 'to weave').

One day, while they were in a seminar, Stéphane Fernandez asked Thomas Roussel this question: if you had only a few hours to present Eskrima to a work group, what would you choose to teach? After thinking a little about it, Thomas answered with certainty: Doble Baston. Among the great variety of techniques mastered in the Filipino Martial Arts, it is certainly one of the most specific and... fascinating — for its efficiency, its speed and its aesthetics.

In a first level of understanding, the faculty to fight with a weapon in each hand gives a considerable advantage, in an offensive way as in a defensive way. Bruce Lee, Kick Ass, Orlando Bloom (Legolas) or even Donnie Yen (Ip Man) show, for that matter, admirable examples in epic scenes in movies. Armed with two sticks or two machetes, it is an impressive technique, raised to a high degree of development in the FMA.

But in the learning process of martial arts, we should always consider the different aspects of our practice, and it never resumes to just one. Because Doble Baston finds a significantly larger application as it allows to develop, with much efficiency, the coordination of the two hands (arms), the symmetry and the ambidexterity of the eskrimador. While learning to overcome the difficulty of manipulating two weapons at the same time, and gaining ease, the eskrimador will also be much more efficient with his bare hands or with one weapon and an empty hand. Likewise, injured or laden, he can use his secondary hand with as much efficiency as with his leading one.

Backed by his mastering of Sinawali, and thus of his body in space, the eskrimador cannot hurt himself or get in his own way anymore. Each arm knows his place to let the other one work.

I. Drills

As in Solo Baston we train again drills, pedagogic exercises with a partner, among the fundamental exercises to develop the martial qualities described above.

A correction in comparison of the Solo Baston (that will then enrich the training with only one weapon), is that two fundamental parameters are to be considered. One part is that the eskrimador focuses on the angle and the work of the hand that serves and is in his visual field. But he must also integrate, at the same moment, the position of his other hand and what move it can follow with. The training of the Check in Solo Baston was already an 'initiation' to that concept.

In order to have sufficient space to apply two long weapons, the appropriate range in Doble Baston is Largo Mano.

In all the following drills, the partners A and B are facing each other and do in sequence the same moves. So if A serves an angle 6 going through strike, B serves also an angle 6 going through strike and their sticks meet at the halfway point, before following with the next move.

Once the drill is acquired, a variation of the training will be to let one of the partners serve the drill normally, while his partner must protect himself with his left stick against attacks from the left side, and with his right stick against attacks from the right side. Another variation is to let the second eskrimador work freely, following his inspiration, while his partner must stay in the initial drill.

From one exercise we get three. And, in spite of the repetitive aspect of the drill, the focus is put back in the core of the training.

HIGH LOW HIGH

1. Angle 1 [R] Lobtik
2. Angle 6 [R] Witik
3. Angle 2 [R] Lobtik
4. Angle 1 [L] Lobtik
5. Angle 6 [L] Witik
6. Angle 2 [L] Lobtik

VARIATION

1. Angle 1 [R] Lobtik
Angle 1 [L] Lobtik
2. Angle 1 [R] Lobtik
Angle 6 [R] Witik
Angle 1 [L] Lobtik
Angle 6 [L] Witik
3. Angle 1 [R] Lobtik
Angle 6 [R] Witik
Angle 2 [R] Lobtik
Angle 1 [L] Lobtik
Angle 6 [L] Witik
Angle 2 [L] Lobtik

The drill can be done with the feet on the same line (shoulder-width apart), with a static right guard, changing guard each time the acting hand changes (same foot / same hand), or moving freely.

4 Count

1. Angle 1 [R] Lobtik
2. Angle 2 [R] Lobtik
3. Angle 1 [L] Lobtik
4. Angle 2 [L] Lobtik

Variation 1

1. Angle 1 [R] Lobtik
2. Angle 6 [R] Lobtik
3. Angle 1 [L] Lobtik
4. Angle 2 [L] Lobtik

Variation 2

1. Angle 1 [R] Lobtik
2. Angle 2 [R] Lobtik
3. Angle 1 [L] Lobtik
4. Angle 6 [L] Lobtik

variation 1

variation 2

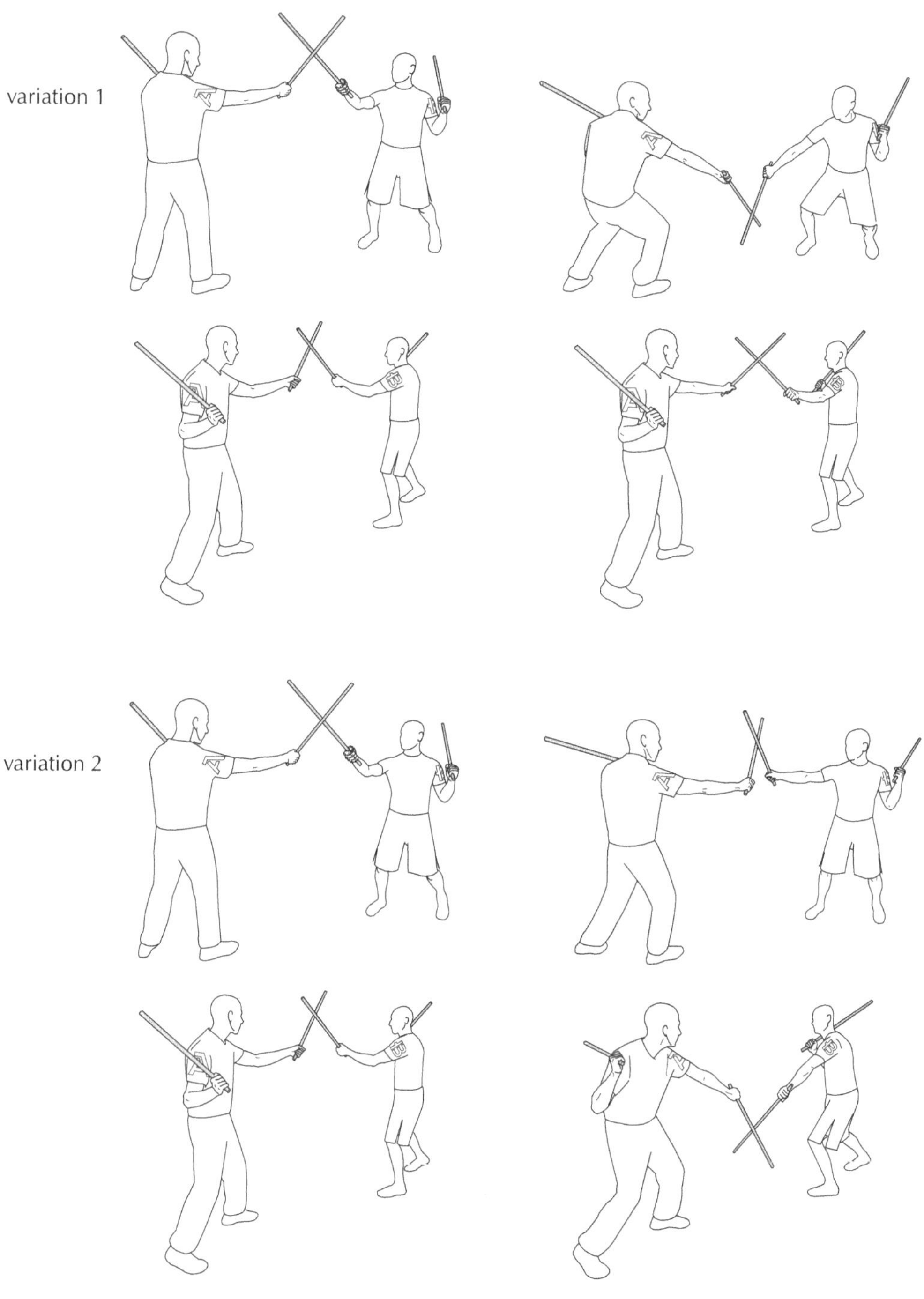

VARIATION 3

Do the three previous variations in sequence. The two partners must stay focused in the present instant to not lose the thread.

5 COUNT

1. Angle 1 [R] Lobtik
2. Angle 6 [R] Lobtik
3. Angle 1 [L] Lobtik
4. Angle 7 [R] Witik
5. Angle 2 [L] Lobtik

6 COUNT / HEAVEN 6

For this count and its variations, the starting guard is:

Right stick above the right shoulder, tip towards the back (Punyo towards the partner)

Left stick under the right arm, tip towards the back

HEAVEN 6

1. Angle 1 [R] Lobtik, the stick goes above the left shoulder
2. Angle 2 [L] Lobtik, the stick goes to the left side, leaving space for the next move of the right stick
3. Angle 2 [R] Witik, the stick goes under the left arm, tip towards the back
4. Angle 1 [L] Lobtik, the stick goes above the right shoulder
5. Angle 2 [R] Lobtik, the stick goes to the right side, leaving space for the next move of the left stick
6. Angle 2 [L] Witik, the stick goes under the right arm, tip towards the back

HEAVEN & EARTH

In the previous version of the 6 count, all the strikes are descending (from the ceiling / heaven). In this variation, the movements 2 and 5 are ascending (from the floor / earth).

1. Angle 1 [R] Lobtik
2. Angle 6 [L] Lobtik
3. Angle 2 [R] Witik
4. Angle 1 [L] Lobtik
5. Angle 6 [R] Lobtik,
6. Angle 2 [L] Witik

Heaven 6

Heaven & Earth

7 COUNT

1. Angle 2 [L] Witik, the left arm goes under the right arm
2. Angle 1 [R] Witik, then passes behind the head to leave the field clear for the left hand
3. Angle 2 [L] Witik, the left arm goes to the left side
4. Angle 1 [R] Witik
5. Angle 6 [R] Witik, the right arm goes under the left arm
6. Angle 1 [L] Witik
7. Angle 2 [R] Lobtik

. . .

8 COUNT

From an open guard
1. Angle 1 [R] Lobtik
2. Angle 6 [R] Witik, the right arm goes under the left arm
3. Angle 1 [L] Lobtik, the left arm goes above the right shoulder
4. Angle 2 [R] Lobtik, while the left stick prepares for the next angle, going from right to left against the chest
5. Angle 1 [L] Lobtik
6. Angle 6 [L] Witik, the left arm goes under the right arm
7. Angle 1 [R] Lobtik, the right arm goes above the left shoulder
8. Angle 2 [L] Lobtik, while the right stick prepares for the next angle, going from left to right against the chest

9 COUNT

From an open guard
1. Angle 1 [R] Witik
2. Angle 7 [L] Witik, while the right hand passes above the head
3. Angle 2 [R] Lobtik, while the left hand passes above the head
4. Angle 2 [L] Lobtik
5. Angle 1 [R] Lobtik
6. Angle 6 [R] Lobtik
7. Angle 1 [L] Lobtik, the stick goes above the right arm
8. Angle 7 [R] Witik
9. Angle 2 [L] Lobtik

In fact, only the first four moves are new in this drill. The last five moves being those of the 5 Count...

10 COUNT

Starting position: left stick held ahead of you, at mid-height, parallel to the floor, right stick in low position, tip towards the front
1. Knock together the sticks, at contact roll the right stick, as in an Arko move, to pass over the left stick
2. Angle 1 [R] Lobtik
3. Angle 2 [R] Witik
4. Angle 2 [L] Lobtik
5. Angle 2 [R] Witik
6. Knock together, at contact roll the left stick over the right stick
7. Angle 1 [L] Lobtik
8. Angle 2 [L] Witik
9. Angle 2 [R] Lobtik
10. Angle 2 [L] Witik

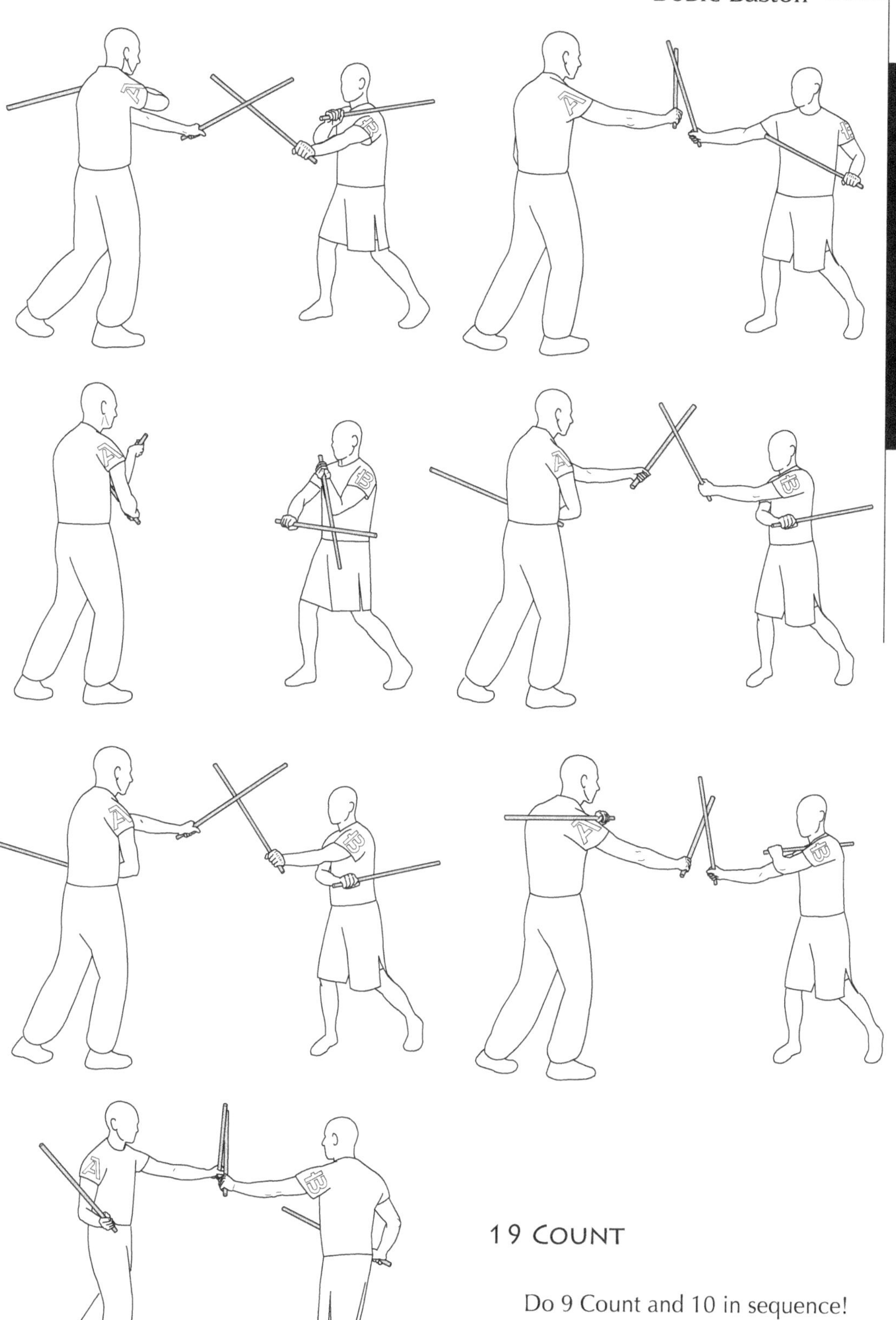

19 Count

Do 9 Count and 10 in sequence!

CRUZADA

Start at Largo Mano range, A and B feet together, sticks crossed in low position
Moving at 45° on the right while winding on: the right stick, high position, tip towards the partner; the left stick in contact with the stick of the partner.
1. Hit like a whiplash with the right stick while pivoting the body. The left stick goes under the right arm, tip towards the back.
2. Angle 2 [L]
3. Angle 7 [R] while lowering the stand, the left stick under the right arm
4. Angle 6 [L]
5. Stand up. Angle 1 [R], the left stick under the arm
6. Angle 2 [L]
A and B go back to the center, feet together, the left hand at the level of the abdomen, the right hand at the level of the head
Moving at 45° on the left while winding the sticks on with a clockwise move
7. Angle 1 [L], the right stick under the left arm
8. Angle 2 [R]
9. Angle 7 [L] while lowering the stand, the right stick under the left arm
10. Angle 6 [R]
11. Stand up. Angle 1 [L], the right stick under the arm
12. Angle 2 [R]
Back to the center, feet together, sticks crossed in low position

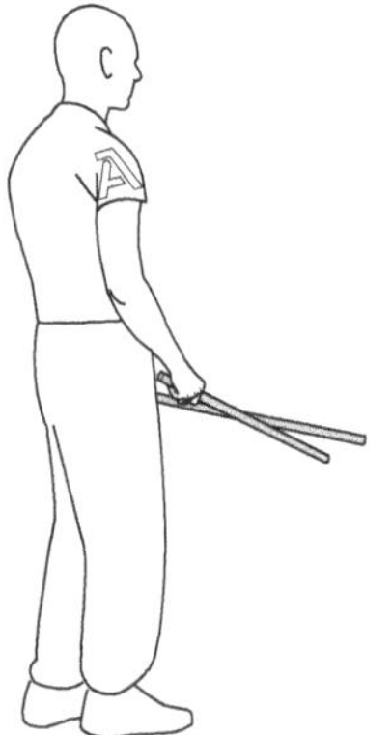

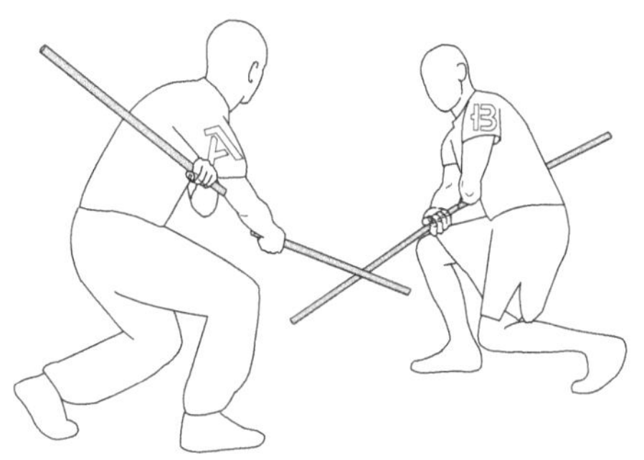
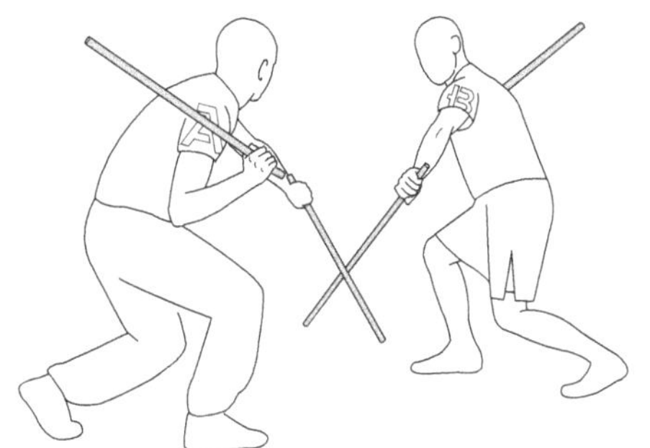

VARIATIONS

One of the partners directs the exercise and chooses how many 'right / left' exchanges are to be done on each side. In the previous drill, they were three on the right side and three on the left side. But we can play with 2, 3, 4 or 5… while alternating high and low.

We can also play with the levels. So, instead of serving an angle 1 [R] followed by an angle 2 [L], we will do angle 1 [R] and angle 6 [L] while lowering the stand.

And of course, the work on the left side is not necessarily symmetric with the work on the right side.

The whole idea being to elaborate a game where the partners must stay in the present moment.

II. Crossada, blocks and counters

We are on an application at Largo Mano range where the opponent must do a step in order to hit the body. That allows the eskrimador to have the space to work with his two sticks.

The principle of Crossada is to offer a crossed counterattack. At the moment of the impact the two sticks form a cross. From the point of view of the energy applied to this counter, if the action was continued, one stick goes down and the other goes up. The two weapons move away from each other…

With your partner, while training in a dynamic way, the two sticks stays on the weapon. In combat application, one stick is on the weapon, the other hits the hand that holds it.

If A takes care to use proper protections, a pair of hockey gloves for example, B can train his hit on the hand in his Crossada.

AGAINST NUMERADO

Largo Mano range
A, Solo Baston, serves Numerado angles 1 to 5
B, Doble Baston, counters with Crossada

The stick on the side from which the attack comes stops the weapon. The opposite stick simultaneously counters on the hand of A (or, in dynamic training, manage the weapon between the first stick and the hand of A). So, against an angle 1 (if A is right-handed, the attack comes on the left side of B), B counters the stick of A with his left stick, and hits the hand of A with his right stick.

Against angle 5, B can choose to counter inside or outside.

When A has served the 5 angles, A and B exchange their roles.

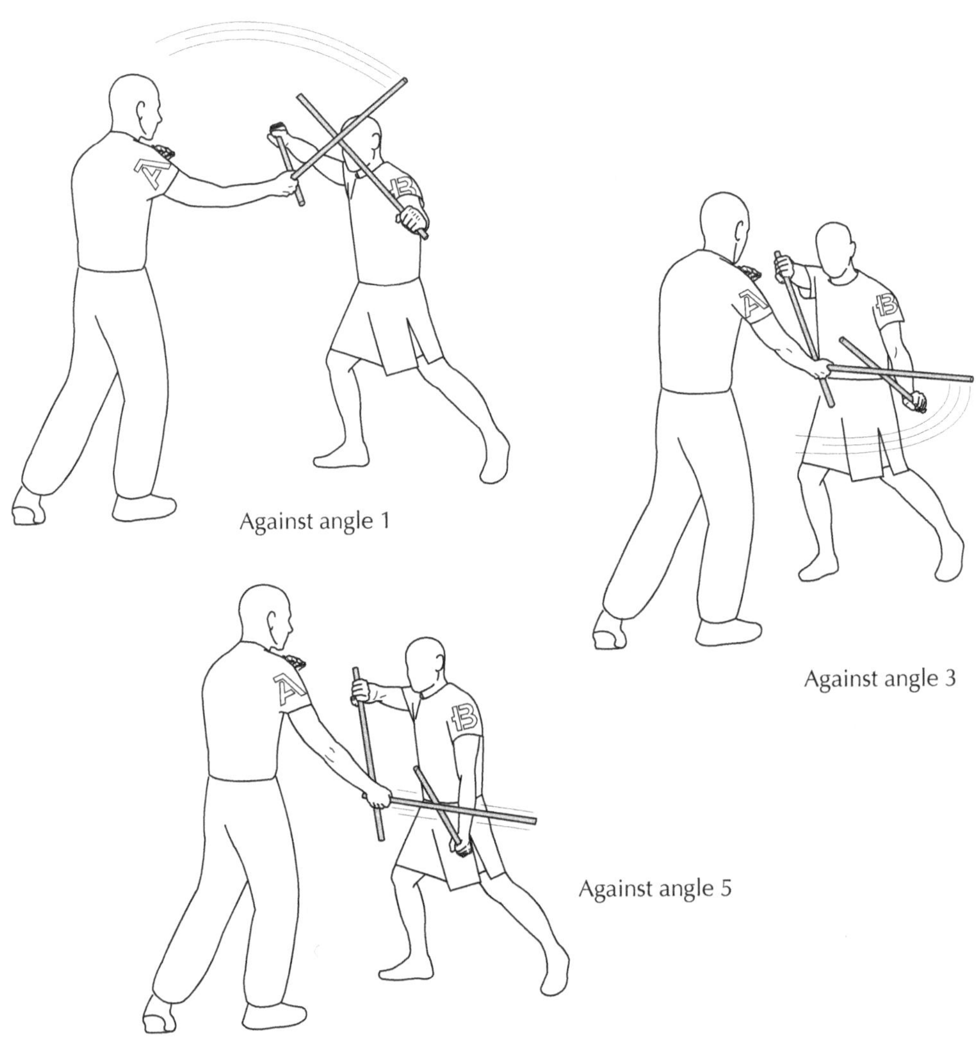

Against angle 1

Against angle 3

Against angle 5

VARIATION 1

Largo Mano range
A, Solo Baston, serves Numerado angles 1 to 5
B, Doble Baston, counters with an opening Crossada and follows immediately with a closing Crossada.

When A has served the 5 angles, A and B exchange their roles.

VARIATION 2: YOUR TURN / MY TURN

Largo Mano range
A, Doble Baston
B, Doble Baston
A serves angle 1 [R] while reducing the distance
B counters with Crossada and goes back to Largo Mano
B serves angle 1 [R] while reducing the distance
A counters with Crossada and goes back to Largo Mano
A serves angle 2 [R] while reducing the distance
B counters with Crossada and goes back to Largo Mano
B serves angle 2 [R]…

VARIATION 3

Largo Mano range
A, Doble Baston
B, Doble Baston
A serves the angles 1 to 5 but in a free order with his weapon held in the right hand, or the one in the left hand
B counters with Crossada

VARIATION 4

Largo Mano range
A, Solo Baston
B, Doble Baston
A serves angles from 1 to 5
B counters with Crossada (opening or closing)
Then counterattack to the arm or to the body with the opposite Crossada (closing if he has chosen to counter in opening…)
And he follows with three strikes to the body, alternating right and left, and the levels

When A has served all the angles, they exchange their roles.

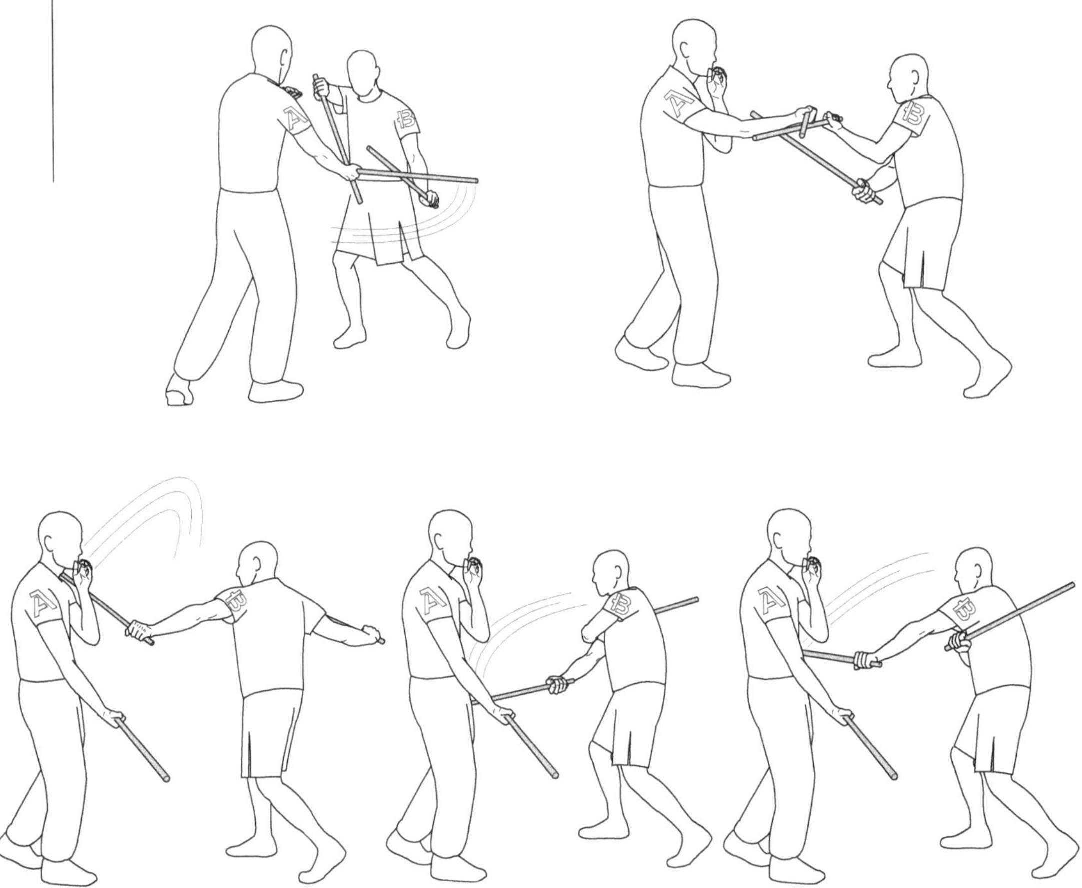

Variation 5

We deliberately train at Medio Contrada range, in order to put ourselves in a difficult position.

If Crossada is a crossed defense where the sticks move away from each other, Palis is a technique where the two weapons are parallel. As previously, the stick on the side where the attack comes does the block on the weapon, the other stick hits the hand that holds the weapon.

On a principle 'your turn / my turn', each one serves the angles 1 to 5. For that exercise the defender chooses to counter using Crossada or Palis.

Medio Contrada range
A serves angle 1 [R]
B counters with Crossada or Palis
B serves angle 1 [R]
A counters with Crossada or Palis
A serves angle 2 [R]
B counters with Crossada or Palis
B serves angle 2 [R]
A counters…

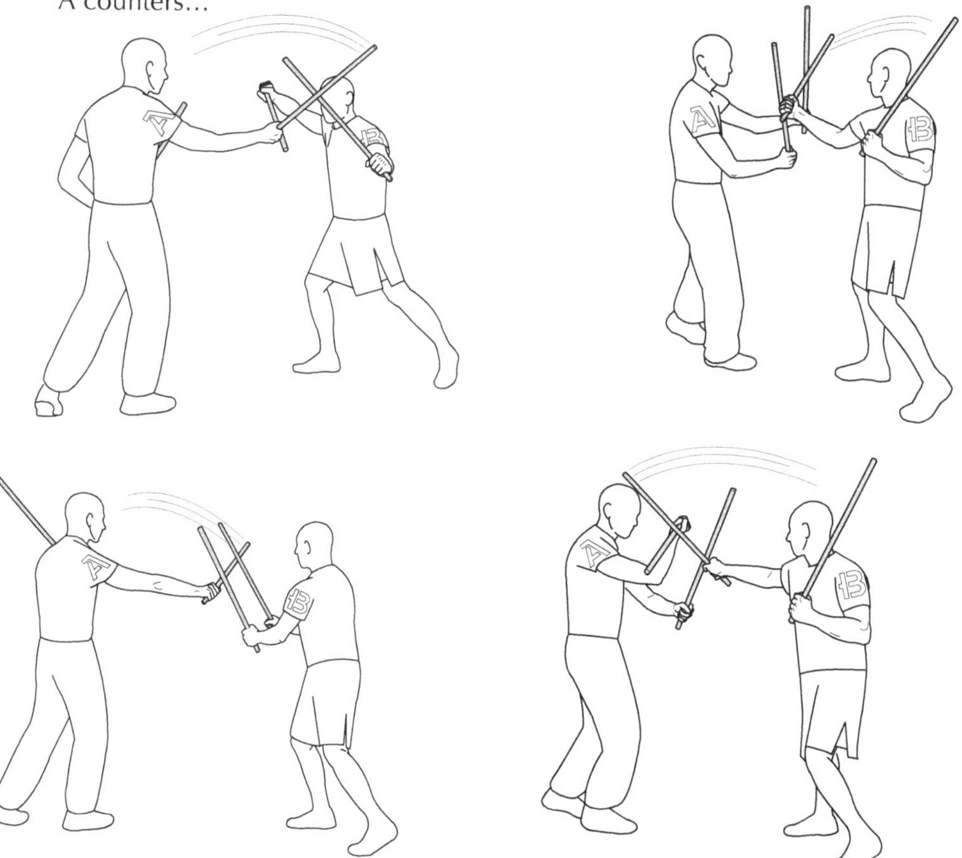

VARIATION 6

The assailant serves the numerado from 1 to 5 with his right stick, but inserts a thrust with his left stick between each angle.

Medio Contrada range
A serves angle 1 [R]
B counters with Crossada or Palis
A serves an angle 5 thrust [L]
B deal with that attack with his closest hand
A serves angle 2 [R]
B counters with Crossada or Palis
A serves an angle 5 thrust [L]
B deals with that attack with his closest hand
A serves angle 3 [R]
B counters…

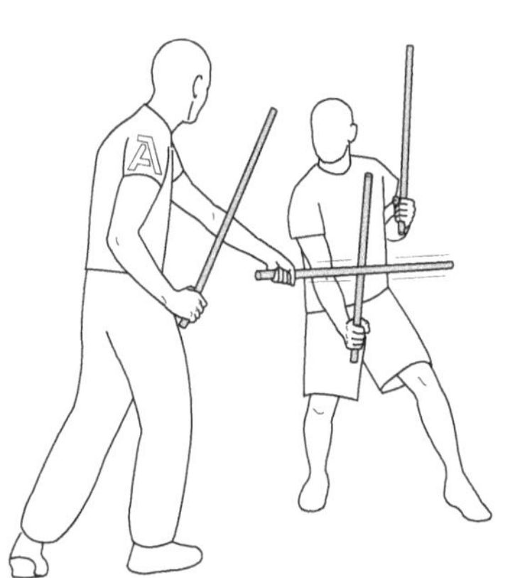
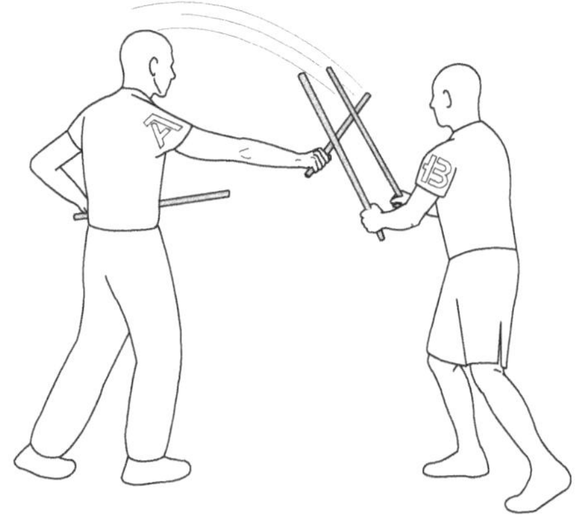

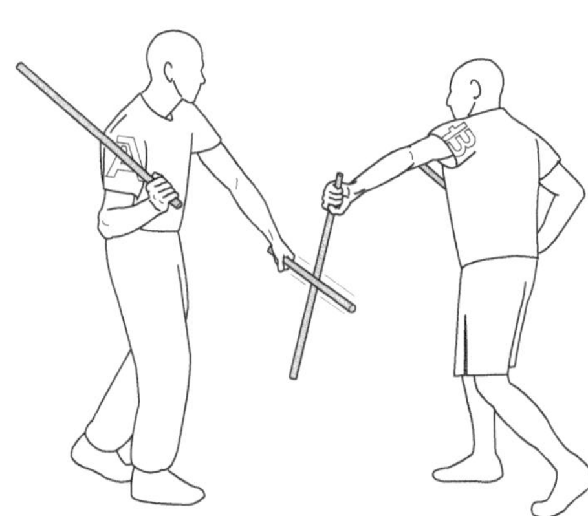
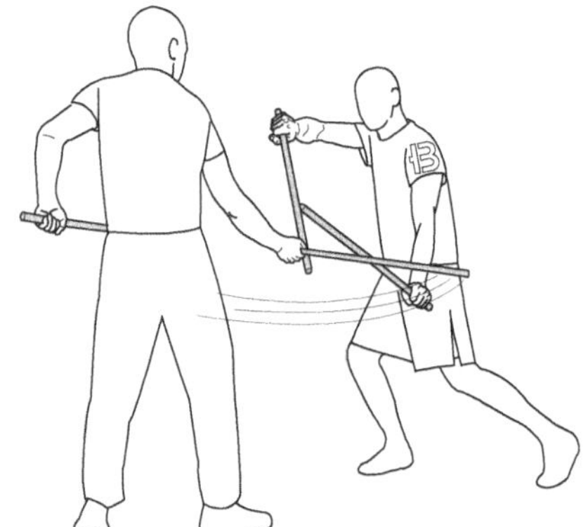

III. Disarms

As in Solo Baston, the disarm is isolated to work on it, set it up, find bearings and integrate its parameters in order to appropriate it. Then, it must be tested in drills, or applications with the partner in order to better detect the opportunities and use it more dynamically. It is a necessary preliminary training for the disarm to be used with efficiency in combat.

In a combative logic, we do not try to disarm directly, we first strike. Moreover, we always keep in mind that the simpler is often the better. And so, that a hard strike to the hand or the head stay excellent choices to disarm an opponent.

The disarms proposed hereafter are demonstrated against an attack with angle 1. Once acquired, they can be adapted against other angles, with proper adjustments. That training will incidentally allow to improve again the coordination and the ambidexterity of the eskrimador, along with his 'physical' understanding of the mechanics of the disarms. Their functioning stands on the basic principles already seen in the Solo Baston chapter: joint constraints, antagonist forces done simultaneously...

For these exercises A is armed with a stick held in his right hand, B is armed with a stick in each hand.

SNAKE

Medio Contrada range
A serves angle 1 [R]
B counters with palis, left stick on the stick of A, right stick on the hand
B takes control of the arm of A by doing a snake with his stick [L] at the level of the wrist
B finalizes the disarm with a pressure on the forearm of A with his stick [R], tip towards the floor

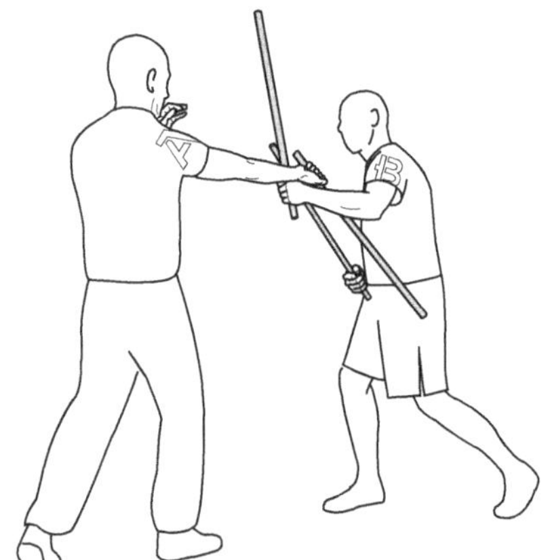

SNAKE 2

Medio Contrada range
A serves angle 1 [R]
B counters with Palis
B takes control of the arm of A by doing a snake with his stick [R] at the level of the wrist
B releases the stick of A by pulling his stick [R] with his stick [L]

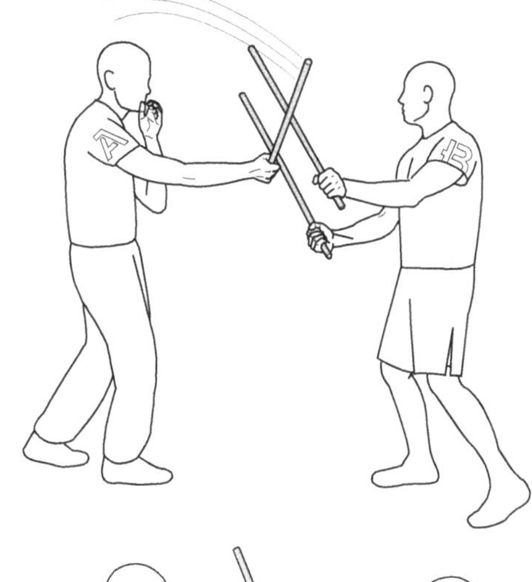

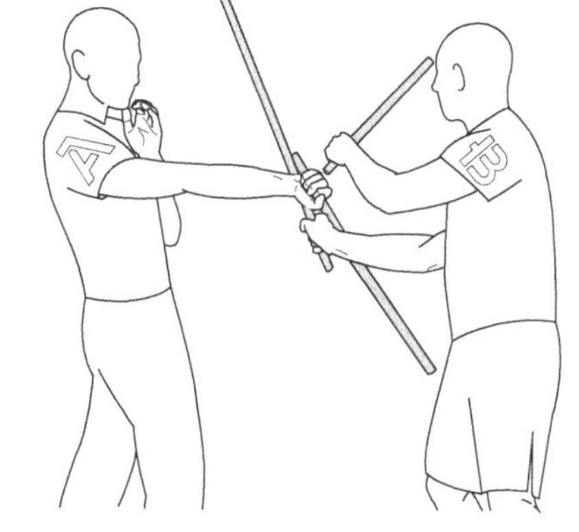

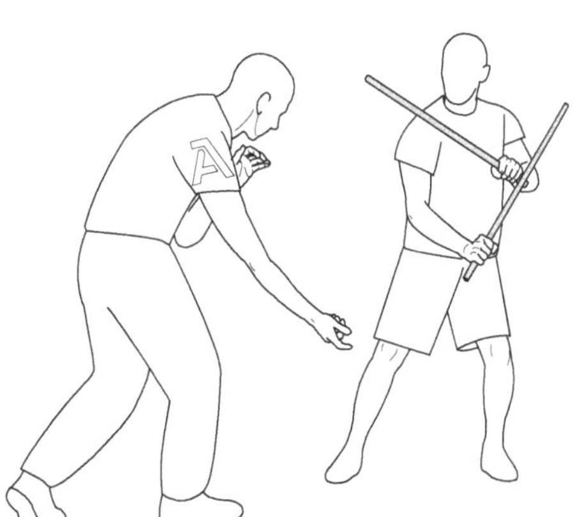

VARIATION

B obtains the disarm by intensifying his lock with his stick [R] counter-clockwise (the stick presses on the wrist of A, the forearm of B presses on the stick of A).
B can simultaneously serve some strikes with his stick [L]

Disarms

PUNYO

Medio Contrada range
A serves angle 1 [R]
B counters with Palis
B hooks the Punyo of A with his Punyo [L] and the stick of A with his Punyo [R]
B finalizes the disarm by doing a clockwise rotation of the two Punyos

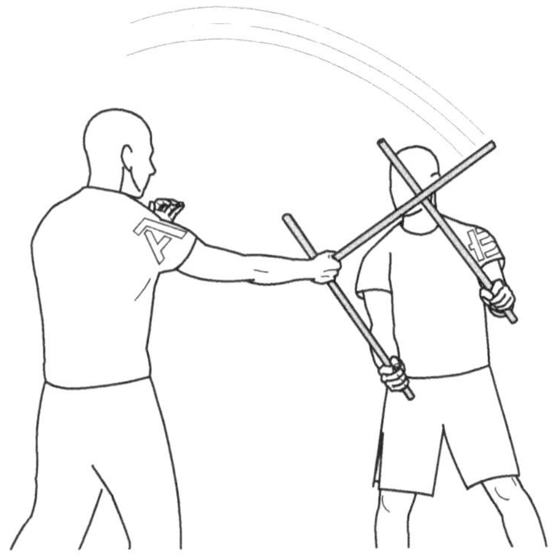

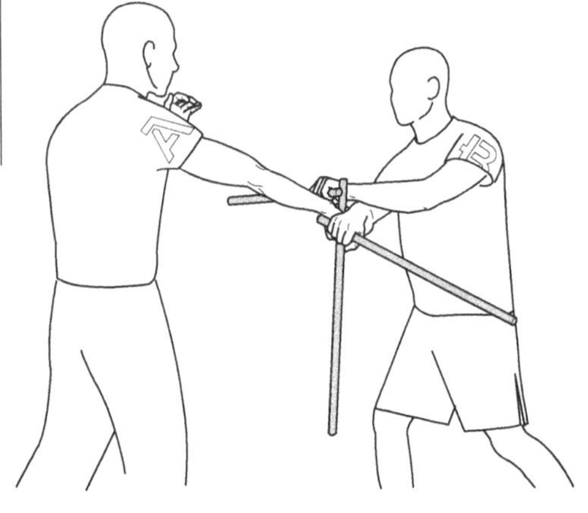

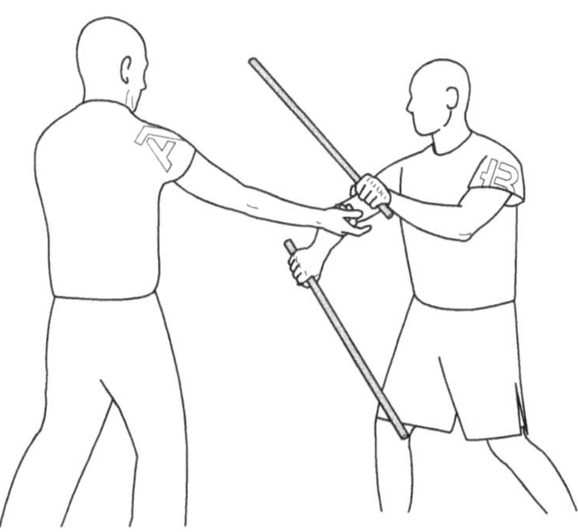

IV. Applications

The Doble Baston applications result from the ease to use two weapons, without obstructing oneself, acquired with the training of drills and Crossada. That ease and that technical quality are incidentally easily transposable to different weapons than sticks — including the natural weapons that are our bare hands.

In the following applications, A is armed with a stick held in the right hand, B is armed with a stick in each hand.

Most of the exercises described hereafter are against an attack on the angle 1, but they can easily be adapted, and must be, on other angles of attack.

Crossada

As seen in the work of Crossada, if the A partner serves a free attack (angle 1 to 7 at his choice), it is possible to counter, even put an end to the exchange, using a stick against his stick and the other against his armed hand.

A is then disarmed or incapacitated, facing B always equipped with two sticks, who can choose to regain some distance or use immediately his advantage with a succession of strikes with his two weapons.

DOUBLE YOUR STRIKES

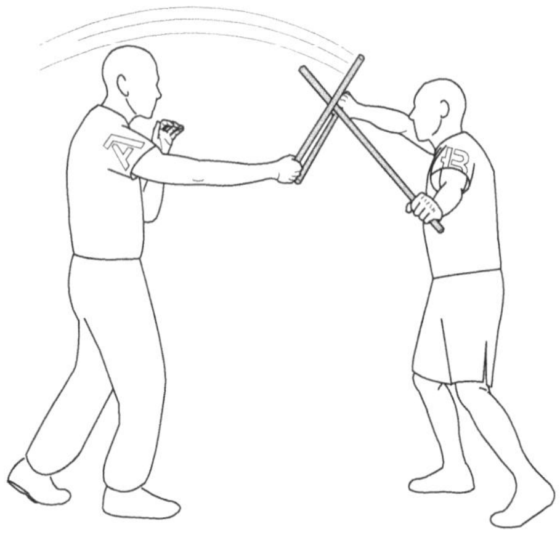

Largo Mano range

A reduces the distance while serving an angle 1

B does a triangle footwork and counters with Crossada or Palis with his stick [L] on the stick of A

B does two strikes in sequence (varying targets, to the torso, to the legs or to the head) with his stick [R]

Then B follows with two strikes to the body with his stick [L]

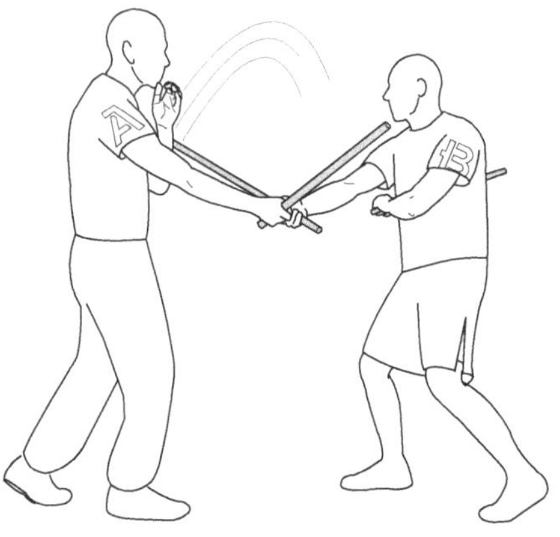

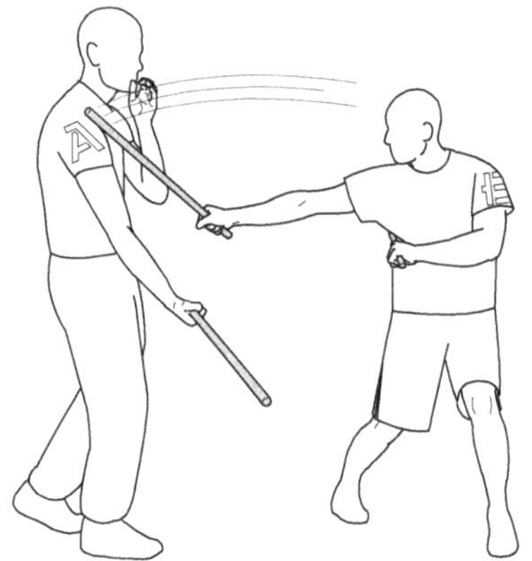

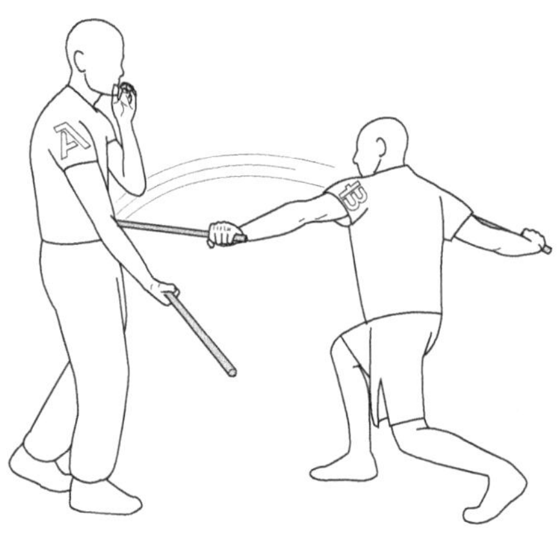

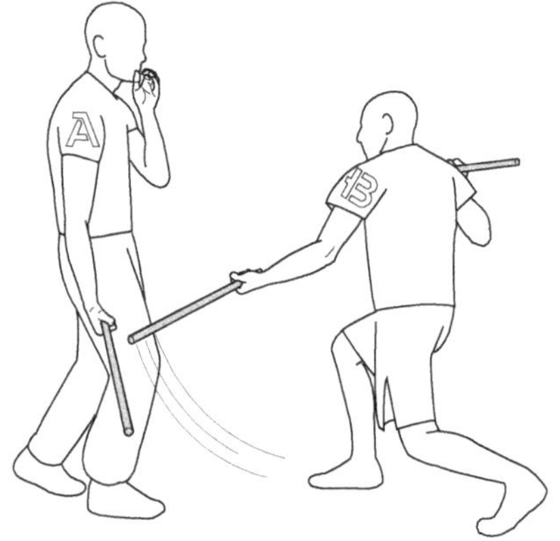

ALTERNATE YOUR STICKS

Largo Mano range
A reduces the distance while serving an angle 1
B does a triangle footwork and counters with Crossada or Palis with his stick [L] on the stick of A
B serves four strikes (to the torso, to the legs or at the head) alternating his stick [R] and his stick [L]

It is important to let the stick [L] in contact with the stick of A, during the first strike with the stick [R].

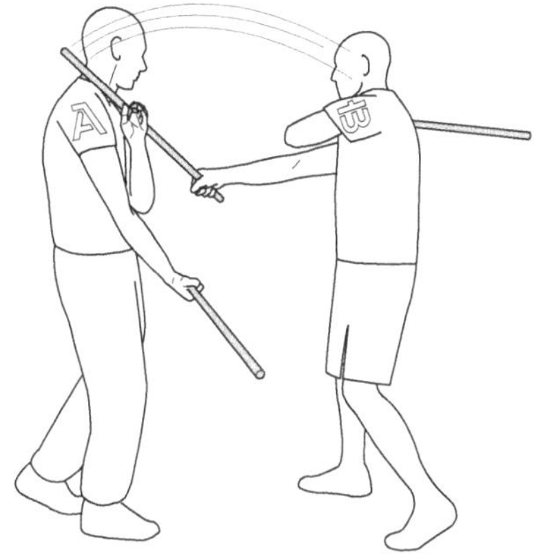

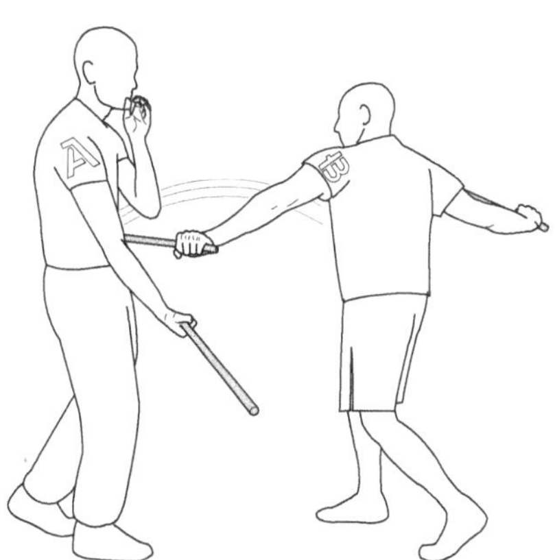

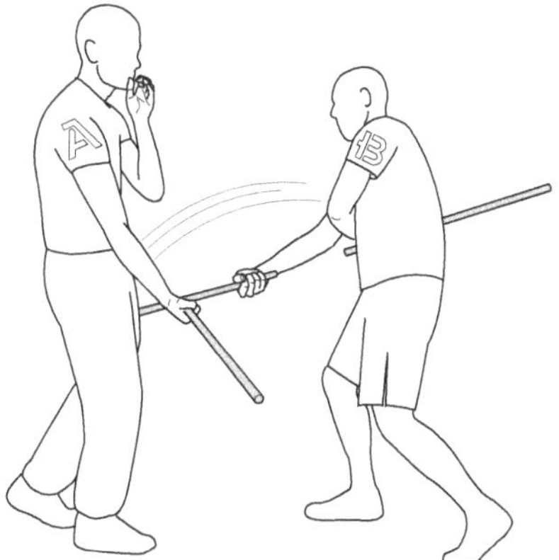

CROSSADA 2

In that exercise the sequence Crossada and Palis is applied to ensure that the armed hand of the partner is neutralized, then followed with free attacks to the body or at the head.

This work will be found again in the counters and counterattacks with knife against knife, where it is imperative to quickly double the cut to the armed arm to ward off the danger of the opposing blade.

Largo Mano range
A reduces the distance and serves a large angle 1
B counters with Crossada, with an impact to the hand with the ascending strike of his stick [R]
B follows with a second strike, descending, to the hand with his stick [R], while his stick [L] has stayed in contact with the stick of A (Palis)
B goes on with an angle 2 Lobtik [R] to the thigh of A
and finalizes with an angle 3 [L] to the flank, an angle 1 [R] to the head and an angle 2 [L] to the head

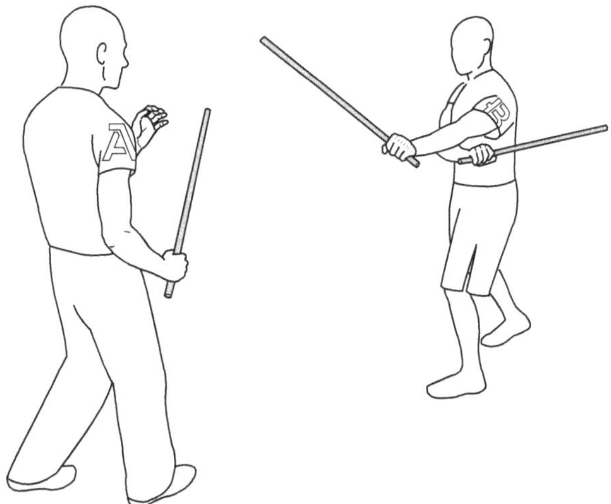

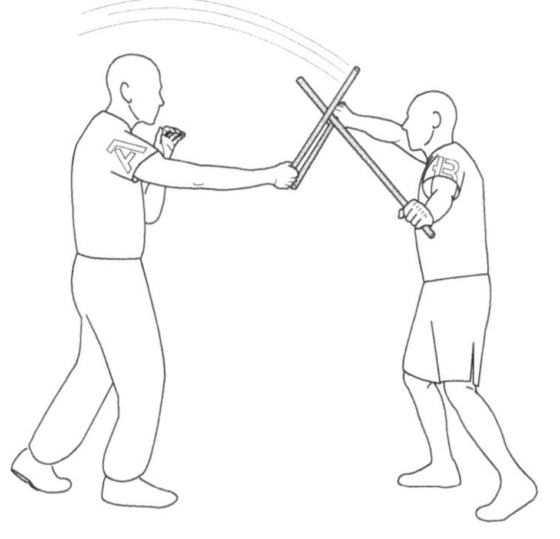
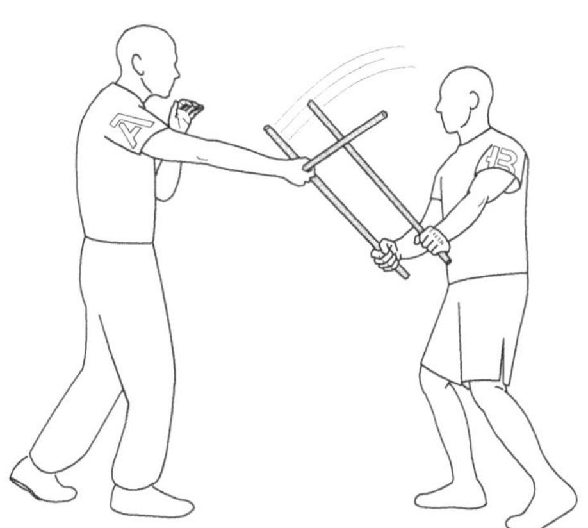

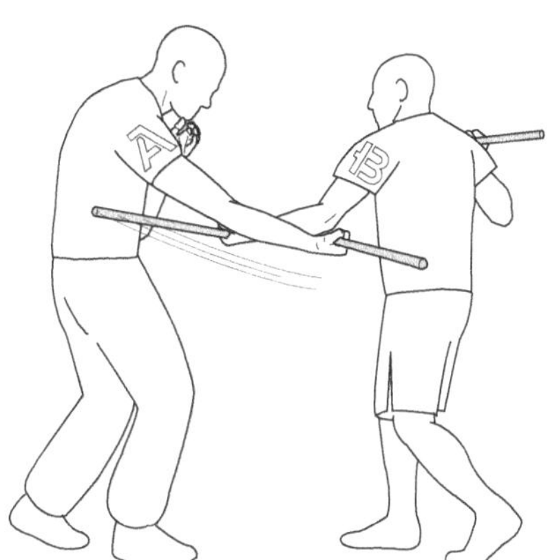
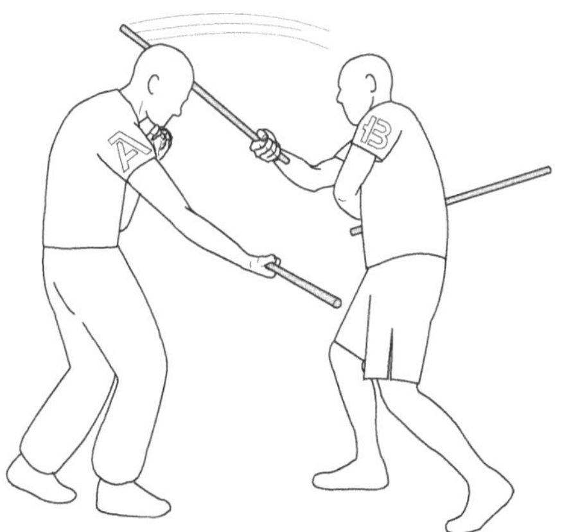

HEAVEN 6 APPLICATION

Largo Mano range
A reduces the distance and serves an angle 1
B does a triangle footwork and counters with the opposite stick [R] from the direction of the incoming attack. His left arm is prepared under his right arm
B follows immediately with an angle 2 strike with his stick [L] at the arm of A
B goes on with an angle 2 strike [R] to the body, an angle 1 strike [L], an angle 1 strike [R]…

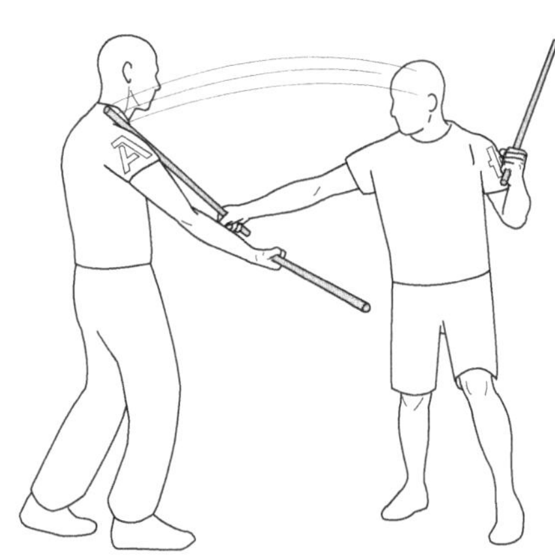

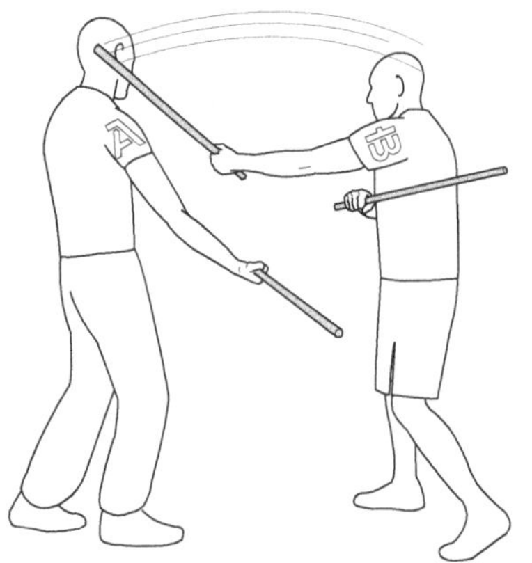

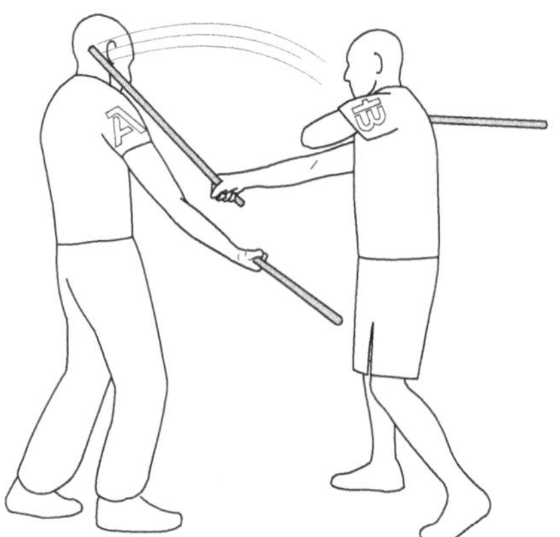

SPARRING

Now that the eskrimador has a knowledge of Solo Baston and Doble Baston, he can spice up his exchanges with his partner: Doble Baston against Doble Baston, Doble Baston against Solo Baston or Solo Baston against Doble Baston.

CARENZA

As in Solo Baston, the training of Carenza, the Shadow Boxing of Eskrima, is one of the best exercises to release the expression and enforce the body ease of the eskrimador.

If the goal is to lead to a free work, flowing, varying the attacks, the angles, the footworks, without an arm obstructing the other... the eskrimador that takes this exercise up often wonders where to start?

In my opinion, a good starting point is the execution of the Doble Baston drills in thin air. It is both a work of memorizing these sequences and a training of the technical qualities with a weapon in each hand.

Once the ease acquired, the eskrimador can start to move, do several drills in sequence, then free himself of the patterns of the drills to reach a free expression.

Knife

The training presented in this chapter is in the order of Martial Art. It allows the eskrimador to get acquainted with the use of a knife, the proper ranges… and with that knowledge, be more aware of its dangerousness and how to defend himself.

Nevertheless, we are clearly beyond the field of legitimate defense as defined by many country laws. It is so strongly advised to the eskrimador to complete that training, in particular by going to seminars proposed by specialists of personal defense.

Because folding or fixed, with one or two edges, the knife is a redoubtable weapon, easy to obtain, easy to hide, easy to apply and highly lethal.

This chapter is in no case an incitement to use a knife or to face it carelessly. It is a technical training which will improve your body mechanics in general, and increase your chances facing a short blade in particular.

For technical training with a partner, we use false knives, made with plastic, wood or aluminum. The tip and the edge are very dulled. For sparring we prefer the Nok model, made with a wooden core wrapped in a compact foam. The eyes are protected by wearing ballistic or construction safety eyewear.

We can of course take on this aspect of the practice independently. But in a logical teaching progression, the eskrimador has first trained the Solo Baston and acquired the fundamentals like angles and footworks. Just like the preliminary training of Doble Baston has allowed him to acquire the coordination of his two hands and the necessary space to work with a blade without cutting himself. So, the base is built, we must now adapt to the specific features of the short blade, cutting and perforating.

I. SLASHES AND STABS

The knife can be held in two different grips, Hammer Grip and Ice Pick Grip. Both of them allows to make slashes as well as stabs.

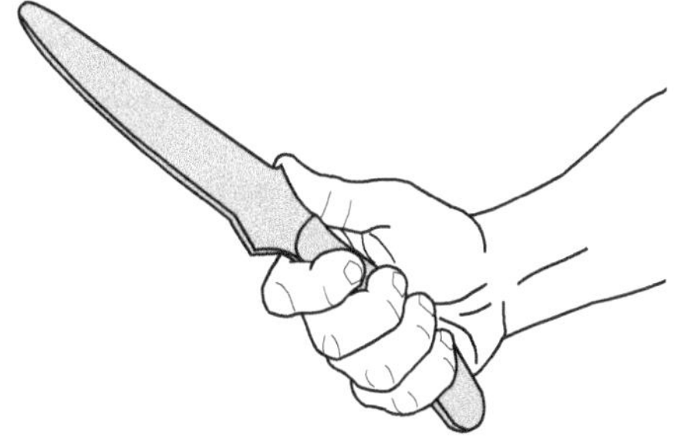
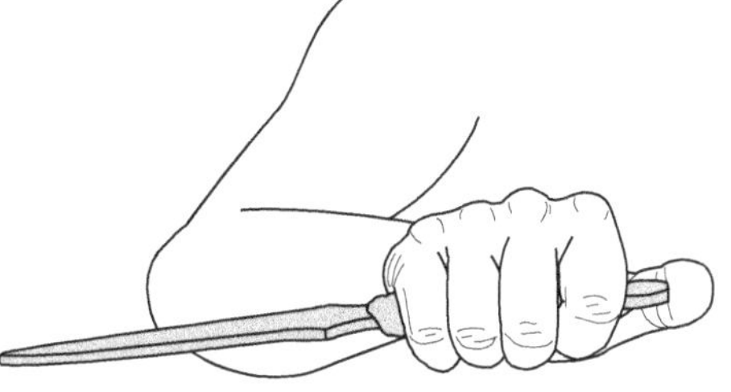

TRAINING ON PARTNER

TWO CHOICE OF SLASHES

We first get familiar with four basic slashes, in the two grips: two diagonal slashes essentially to the throat (angles 1 and 2) and two horizontal slashes to the abdomen (angles 3 and 4). The movement of the wrist must allow the armed hand to stay in line with the forearm. We let the blade slide to feel the cutting effect.

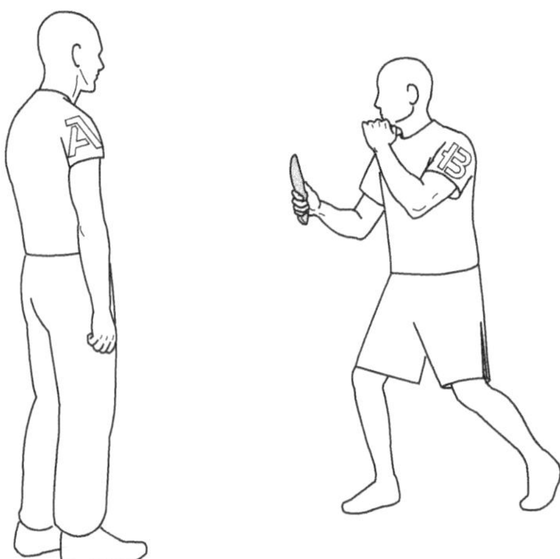

Largo Mano range
A stands straight with his arms at his sides, B is in guard with his unarmed hand protecting his throat
B enters with an half-step, does two slashes in sequence (for example angle 1 slash an backhand angle 4 slash)
B gets out with an half-step
Several times then A and B exchange their roles

We try to do the sequence of slashes with flow, leaving as less as possible the body of the partner. We also vary the angles and try the two grips.

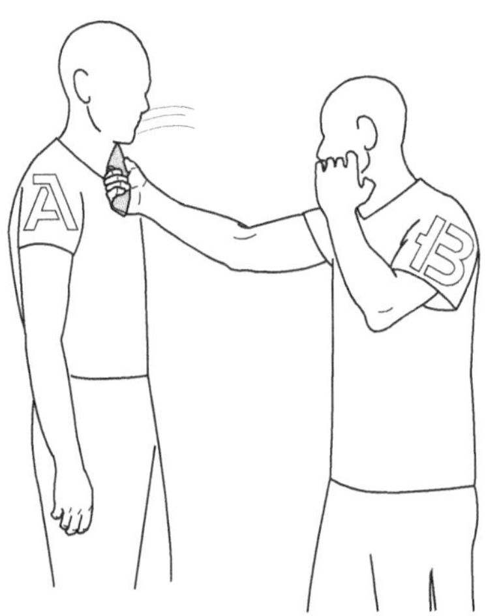

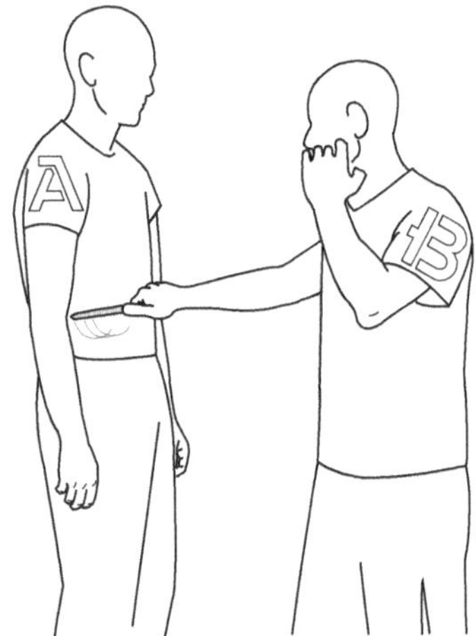

SLASH AND STAB

Same exercise, but we do a slash and a stab in sequence — always complying with the principle to leave as less as possible the contact with the body of the partner. So, we choose angles that follows in a logical order as a descending slash and an ascending stab (angle 1 slash and angle 6 stab for example).

Largo Mano range
A stands straight with his arms at his sides, B is in guard with his unarmed hand protecting his throat
B enters with an half-step and does a slash and a stab in sequence
B gets out with an half-step
Several times then A and B exchange their roles

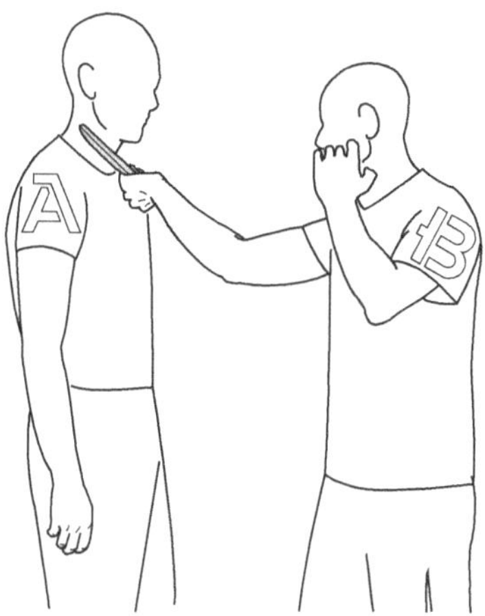 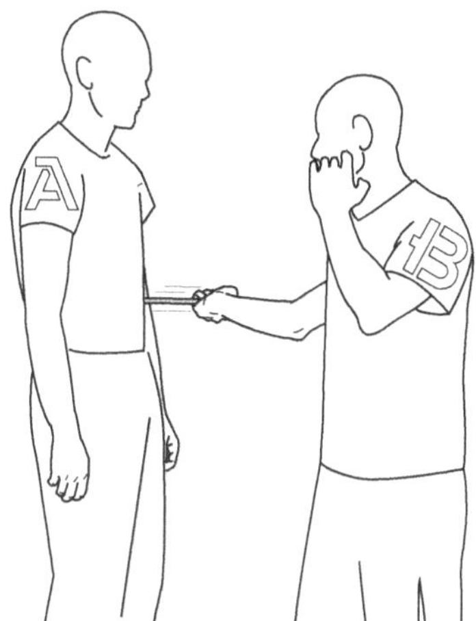

TWO SLASHES AND A STAB

The exercise is identical but we do two slashes before we finalize with a stab. For the latter, we choose lethal targets, avoiding the 'bony armor' that the thoracic cage forms.

TRAINING WITH PARTNER ON NATURAL COUNTER

For the following exercises, A is bare hands, B is armed with a knife held in his right hand. We try the two grips.

STABS 1/3/4/2

Largo Mano range

B enters with an half-step and serves a stab to the throat in angle 1
A makes a natural block by interposing the back of his forearm [L] at the level of the wrist of B
The stab of B transforms into a slash to the throat by a rotation of the wrist, undoing the effect of the block
B gets out with an half-step

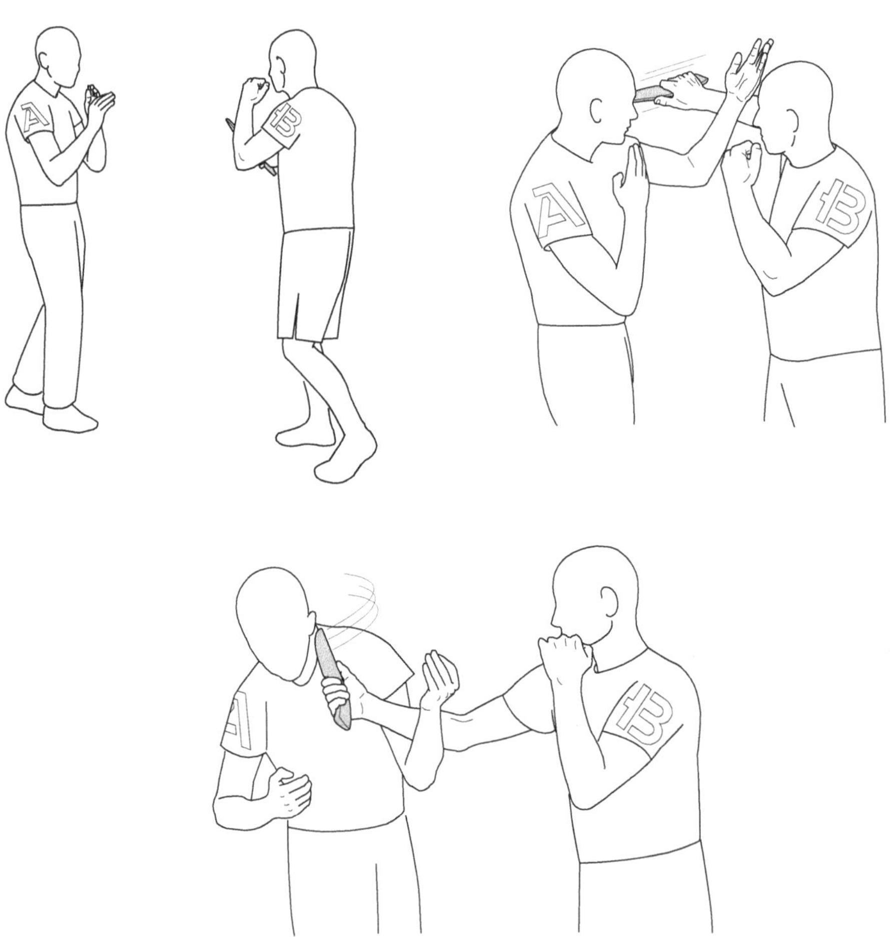

Alternately the slash can be to the arm or to the body. B can also use the back of his weapon to clear the protection of A (open) before cutting.

The natural block is a reflex of who sees the stab attack coming. As soon as there is contact with the defense, the attacker adapts and changes his move to, in the end, hit with a slash.

B does the four angles getting in and out of the range each time.

B enters with an half-step and serves a stab to the side in angle 3
A makes a block with his forearm [L].
B use a move of his wrist or a trapping with the back of his blade to cancel the protection and do a slash
B gets out with an half-step

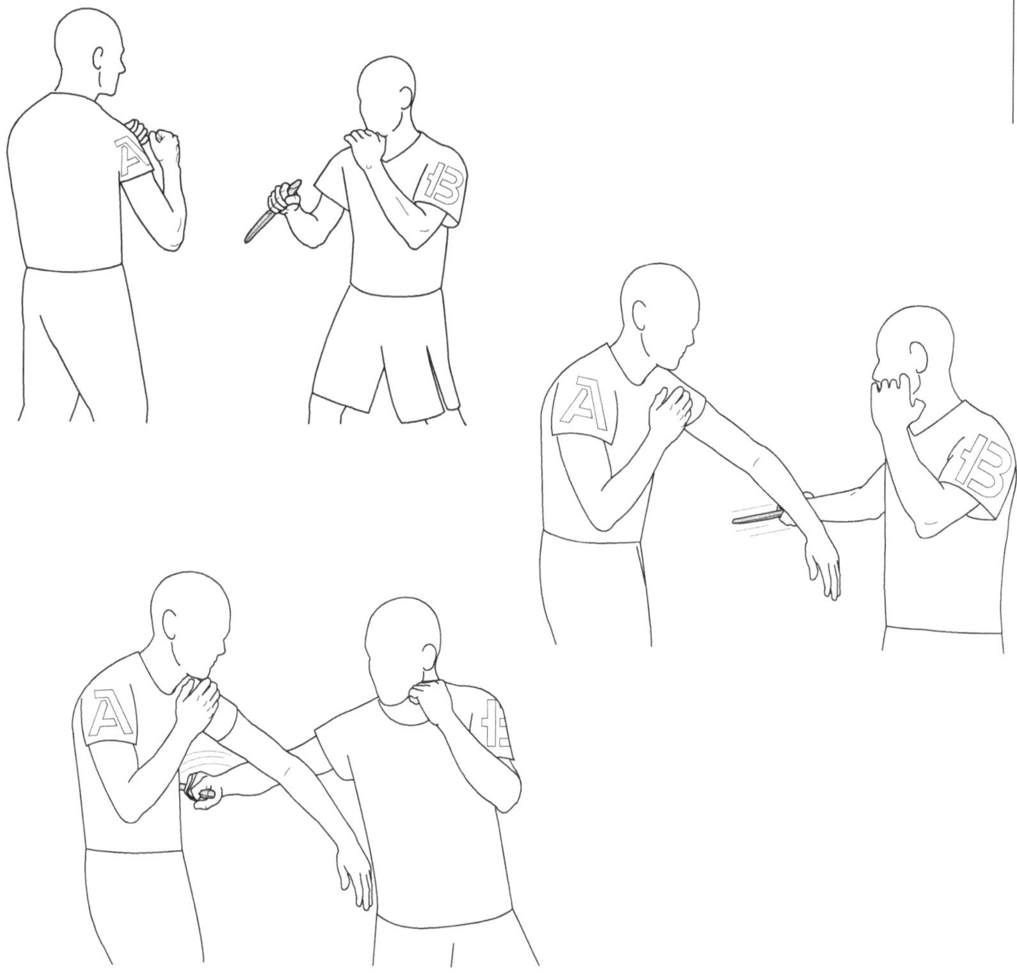

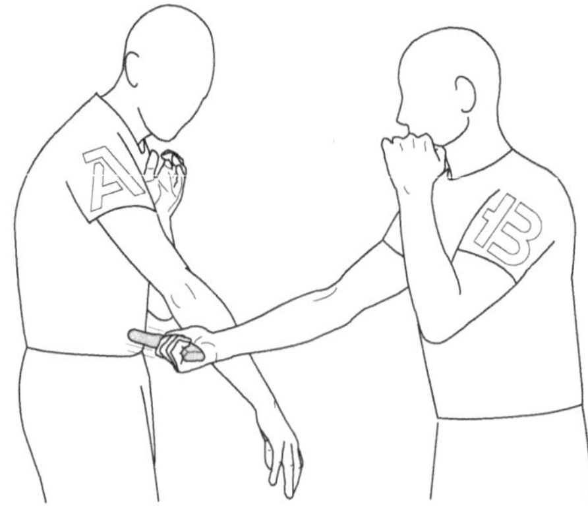

B enters with an half-step and serves a stab to the side in angle 4
A makes a block with his forearm [R]
B cancels the protection and slashes
B gets out with an half-step

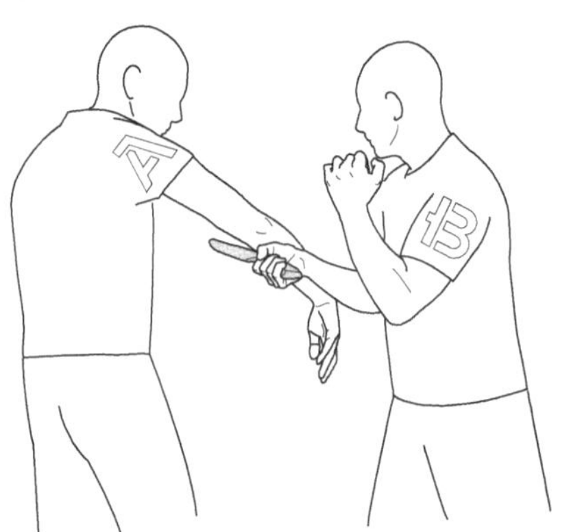

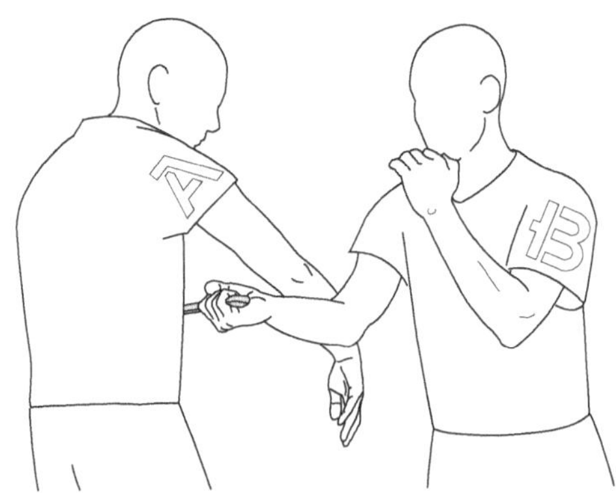

B enters and serves a stab to the throat in angle 2
A makes a block with his forearm [R]
B cancels the protection and slashes
B gets out

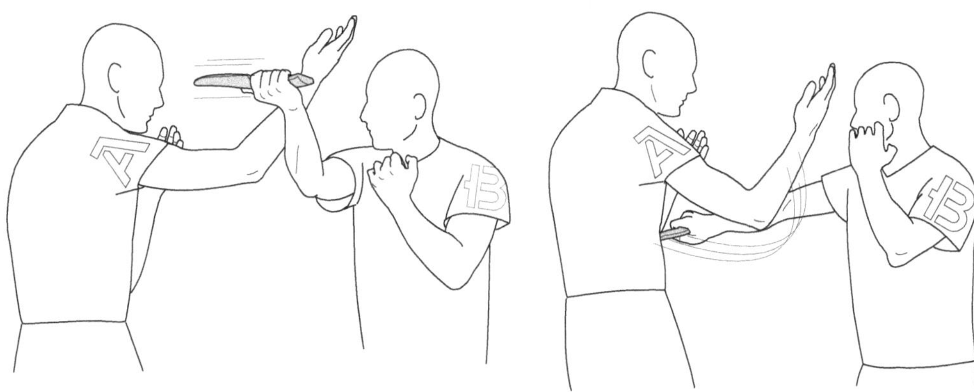

A and B exchange their roles

STABS 1/3/4/2 AND UNARMED HAND

We train again on four attacks in stab while the partner reacts with a natural block, with his arm on the side where the attacks comes.

But this time, the attackers clears the protection using his unarmed hand.

Largo Mano range

B enters and serves an angle 1 stab to the throat
A makes a natural block with his forearm [L]
B gets the arm of A out with a Check of his empty hand at the elbow (from below)
B can now stab to the throat or in the kidneys
B gets out of the range

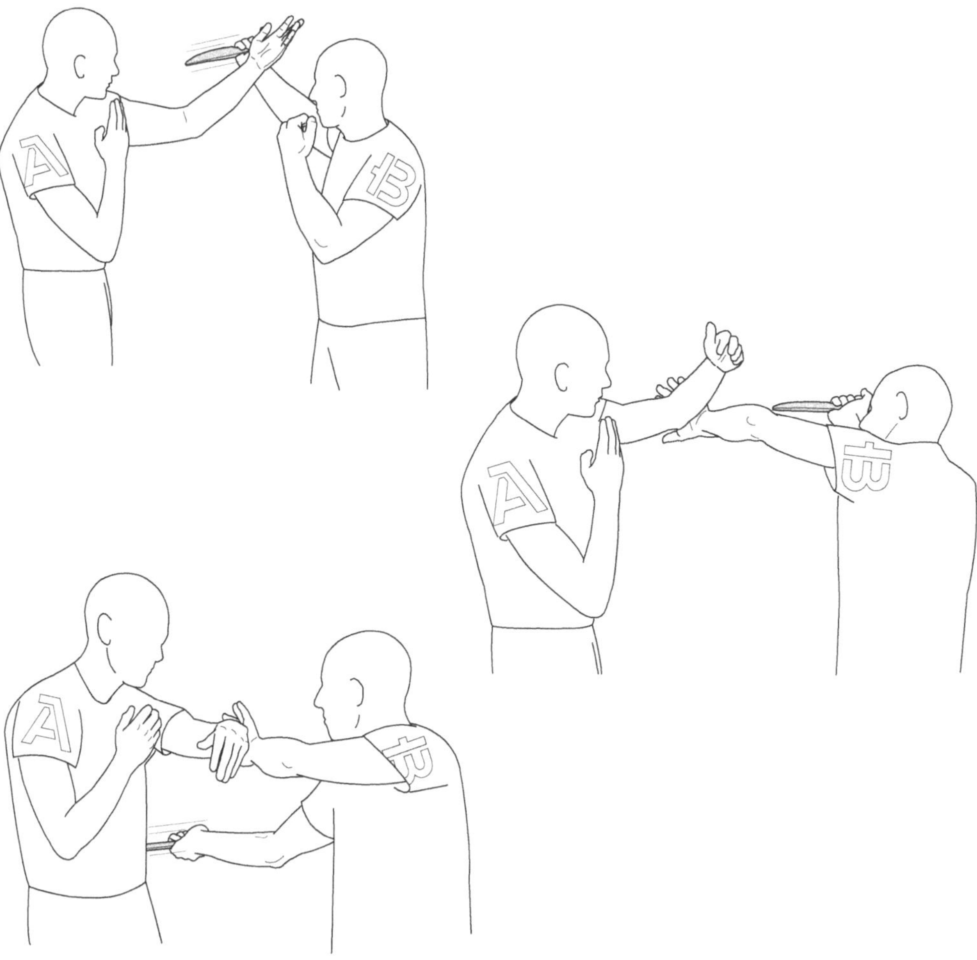

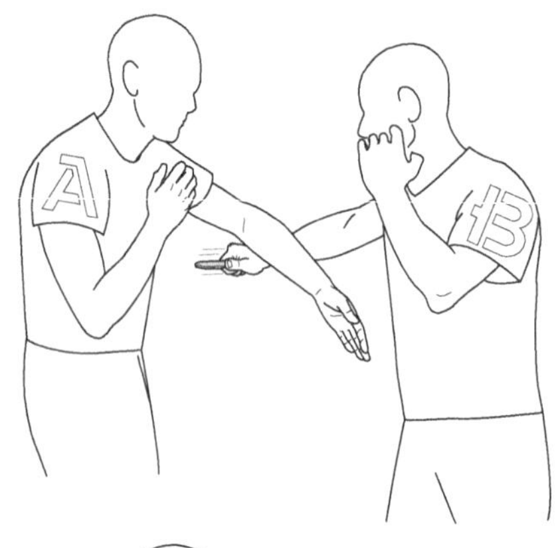

B enters and serves an angle 3 stab to the abdomen
A makes a natural block with his forearm [L]
B clears the arm of A with a Check of his empty hand at the elbow (from above)
B can now stab to the abdomen or in the kidneys
B gets out of the range

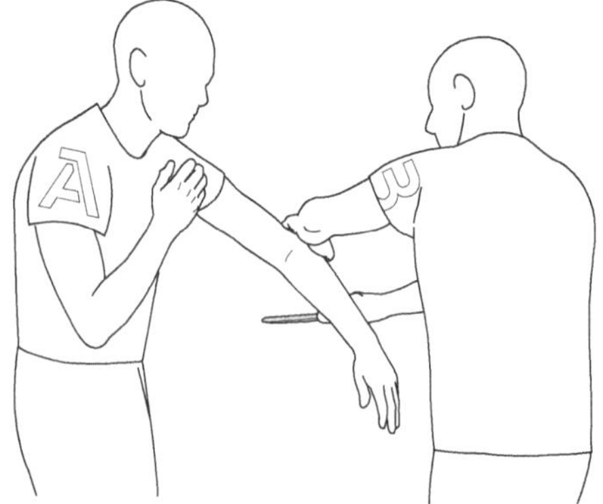

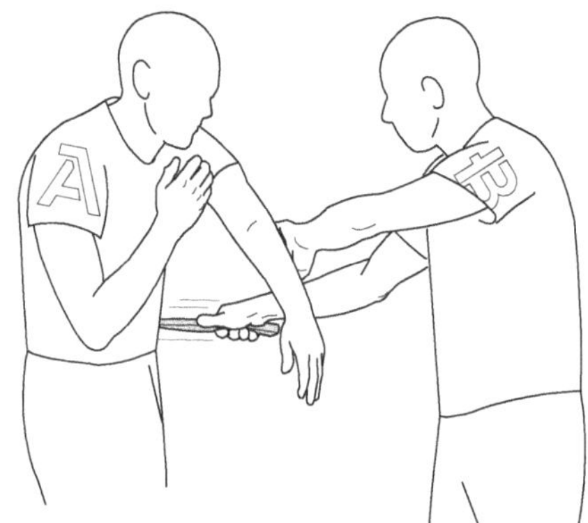

B enters and serves an angle 4 stab to the abdomen
A makes a natural block with his fore-arm [R]
B clears the arm of A with a Check of his empty hand at the elbow (from above)
B can now stab to the abdomen
B gets out of the range

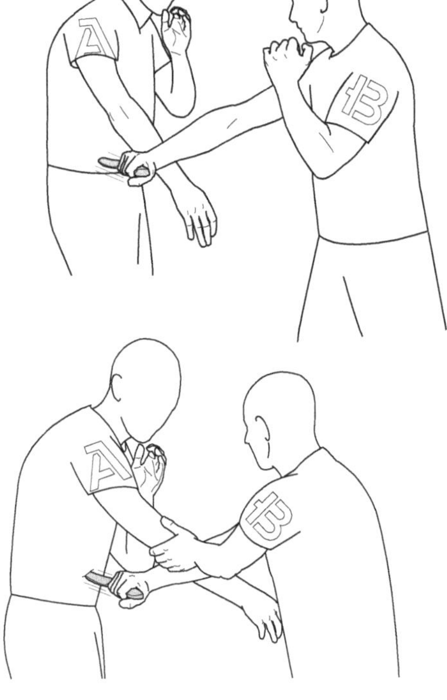

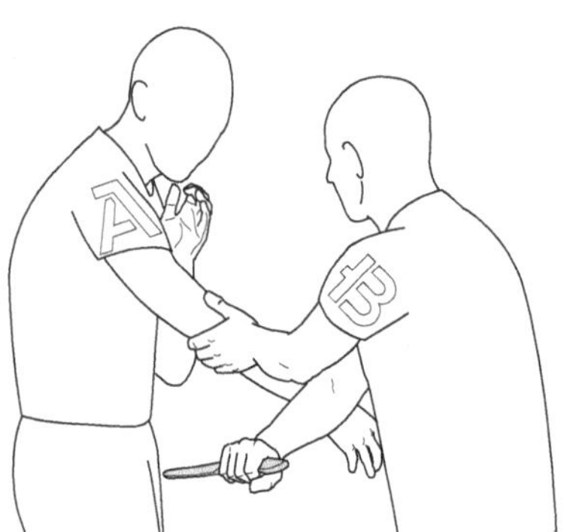

B enters and serves an angle 2 stab to the throat
A makes a natural block with his forearm [R]
B clears the arm of A with a Check of his empty hand at the elbow (from below)
B can now stab to the throat
B gets out of the range

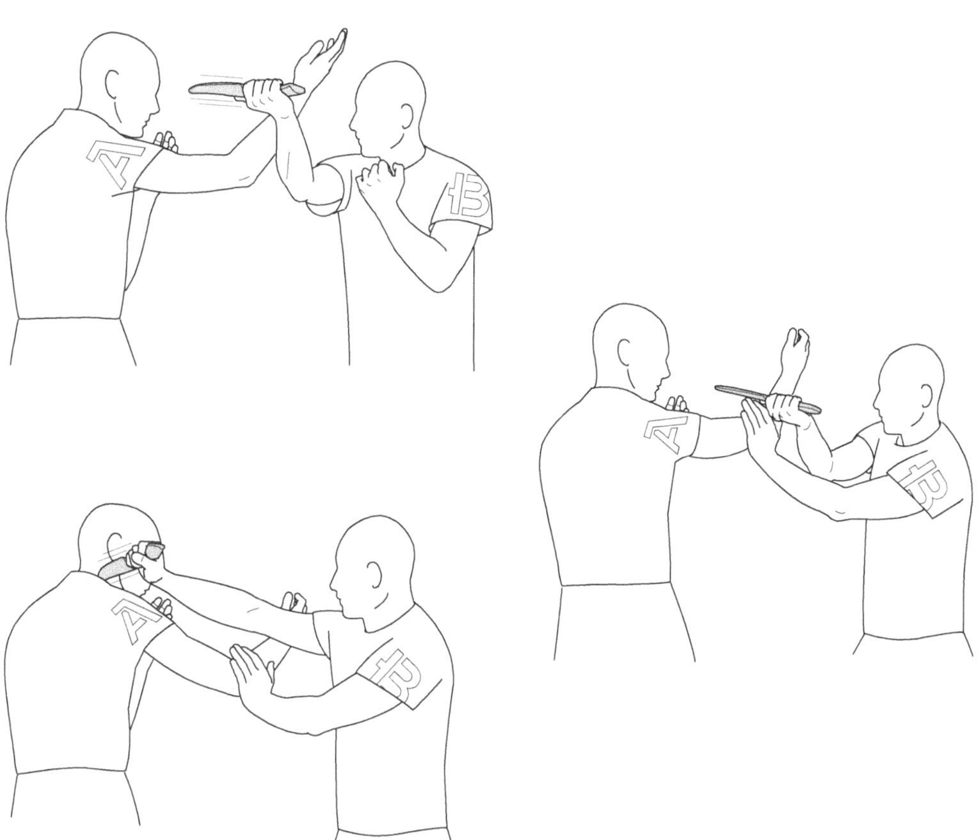

A and B exchange their roles

II. Counters and Counterattacks

To apply a knife when facing a knife allows to equalize the offensive potential, but not at all the defensive potential. We can not use a knife as a shield or to parry. The first among the protections is the security range. So, we will work at the minimum at Largo Mano range in the engagement of the fight. At Medio Contrada, or Corto, which are quite the same due to the length of the weapon, it is almost impossible to be aware of the attacks of the opponent.

However, to insure the dynamics of some educational exercises, we train deliberately at the biased range of Medio Contrada, while keeping in mind that it is a constraint of the exercise and not a coherent range of engagement with a knife.

It is notably the case with the two following exercises where we will work against the five basic angles, and offer immediate counterattacks. While training Solo Baston we had isolated the counters before working the counterattacks. Here, we consider the eskrimador to have already integrated enough of the system to combine both in a dynamic setting.

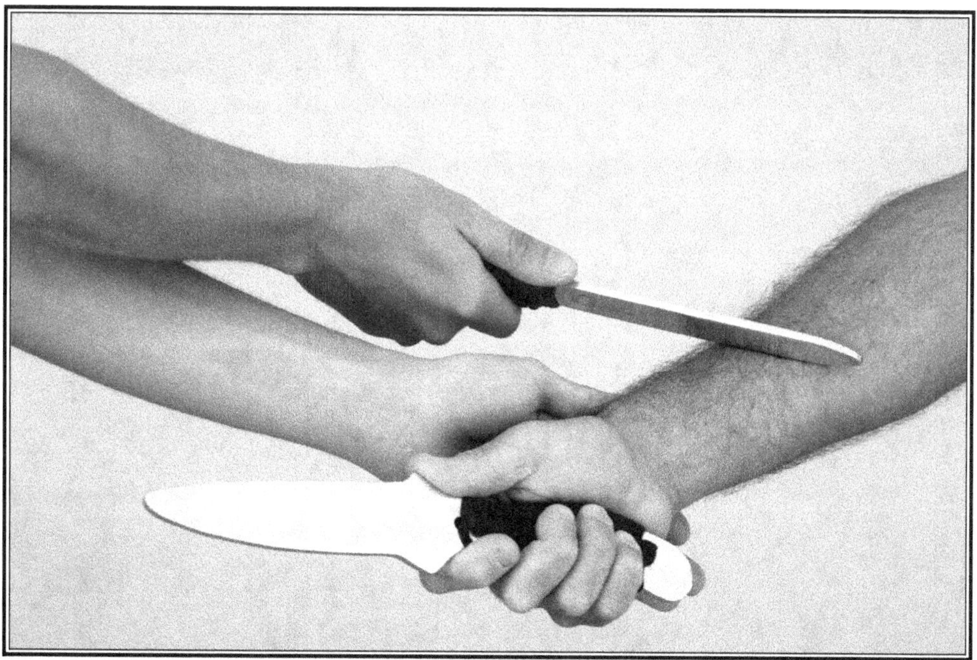

TRADITIONAL EXERCISE

A and B are armed with a knife and hold it in Hammer grip.

Medio Contrada range
A serves an angle 1 slash to the throat
B blocks with his unarmed forearm and does simultaneously an ascending slash in the forearm of A.

We find here again the move of Crossada seen in the training of Doble Baston.

Facing an attack with a knife, the first important goal remains not to be hit. So, we will try hard, while doing the block, to move the targets away (with a step, a pivot and/or a physical exaggeration). We purchase some distance.
The difficulty is, in the exercise, to stay at Medio Contrada range.

B serves a second slash to the arm, descending, and follows with a slash to the side and a stab to the abdomen

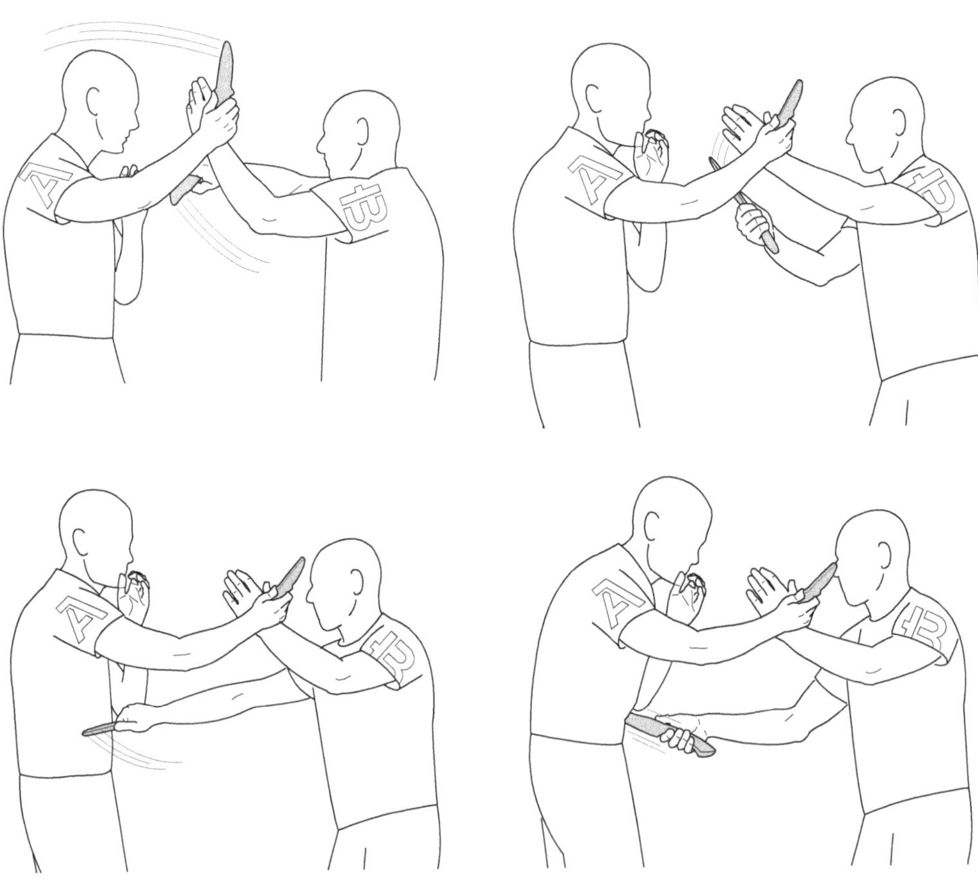

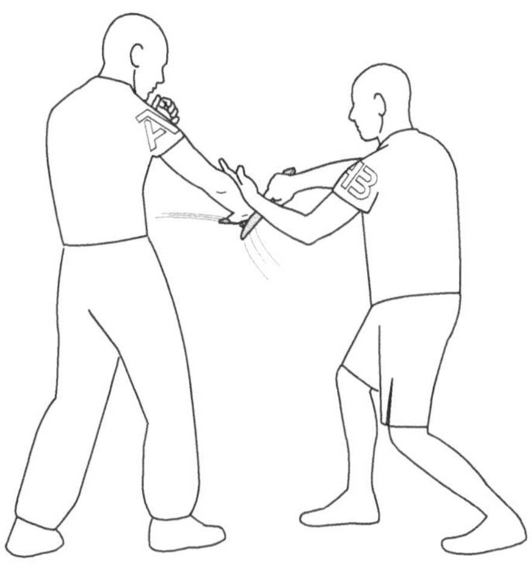

A serves an angle 4 slash to the abdomen
B blocks with his unarmed forearm, while purchasing some distance, and does an ascending slash in the forearm of A
B serves a second descending slash to the arm
B redirects the armed arm of A to open the guard

While redirecting, we take care not to let a part of our body on the way of the blade. In that purpose, we use both our body mobility and a pressure exerted towards the opponent.

B serves two counterattacks to the body, a slash and a stab

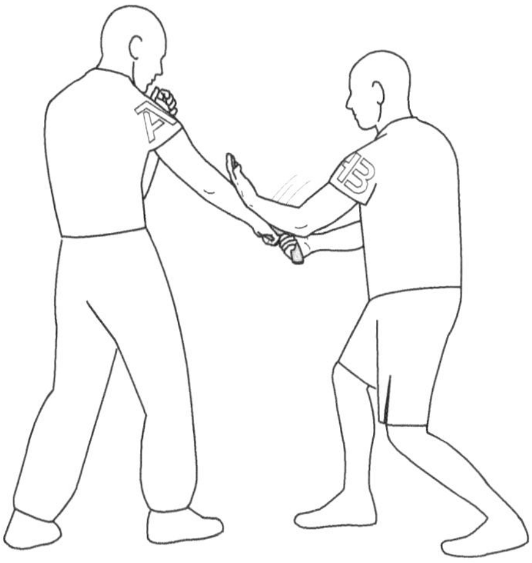

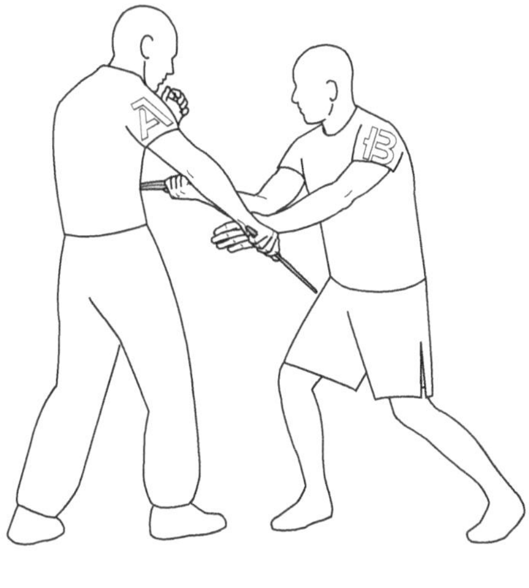

A serves an angle 3 slash to the abdomen
B blocks with his unarmed forearm, while purchasing some distance, and does an ascending slash in the forearm of A
B serves a second descending slash to the arm and follows with two counterattacks to the body, a slash and a stab

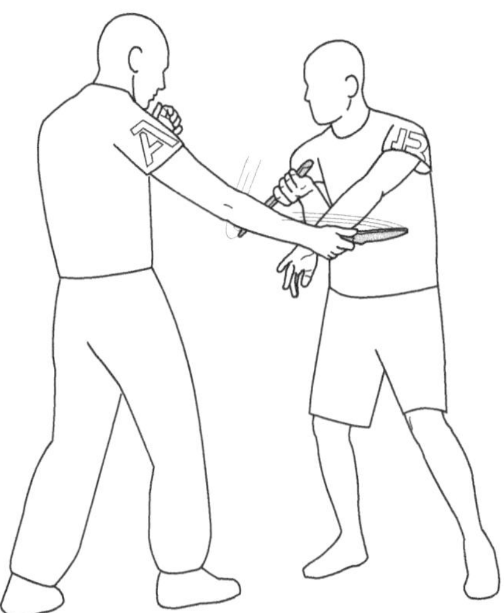
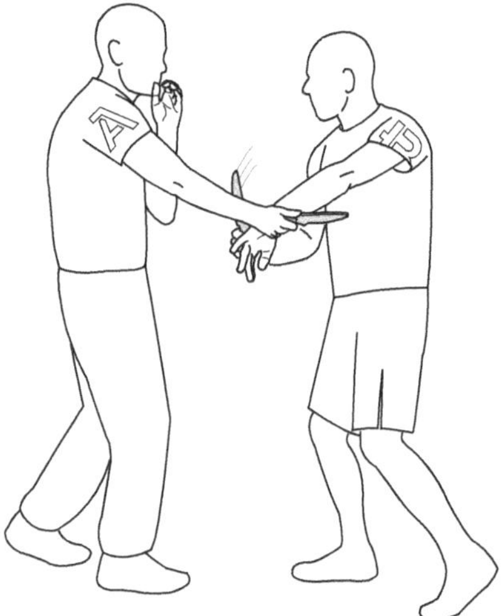
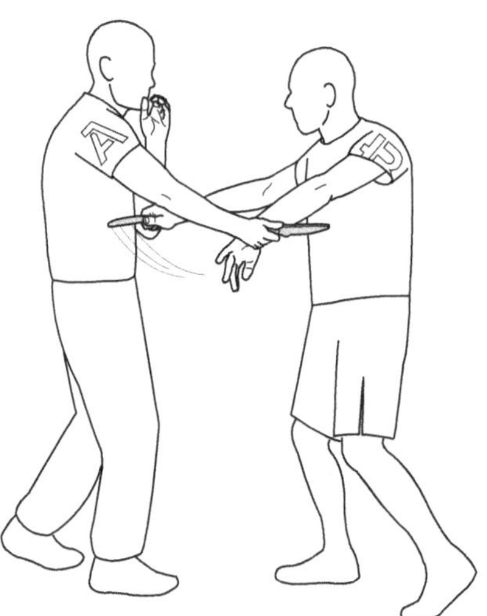
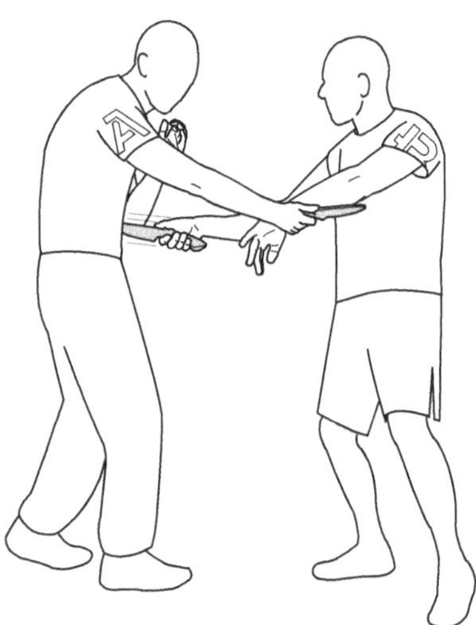

A serves an angle 2 slash to the throat
B blocks with his unarmed forearm, while purchasing some distance, and does an ascending slash to the forearm of A
B serves a second descending slash to the arm
B follows with two counterattacks to the body, a slash and a stab

While cutting in the forearm, we take care not to risk of getting injured. So for the arm, that does the block, not to be in the way of the blade, against angle 1 and angle 3, B does his slash between the hand that does the block and the shoulder of A. Against angle 4 and angle 2, the slashes of counterattack are done between the forearm of B that does the block and the hand of A.

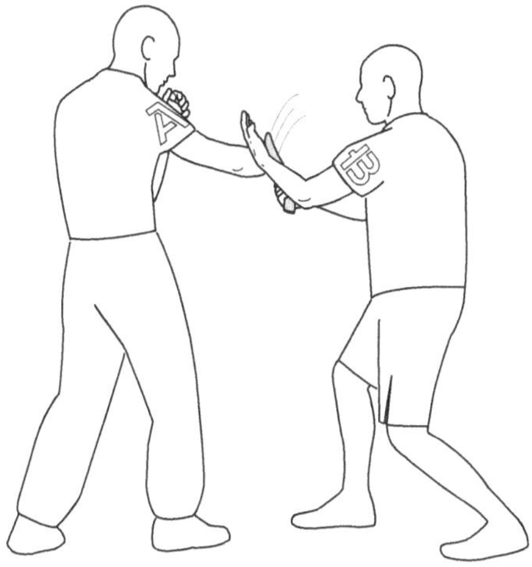

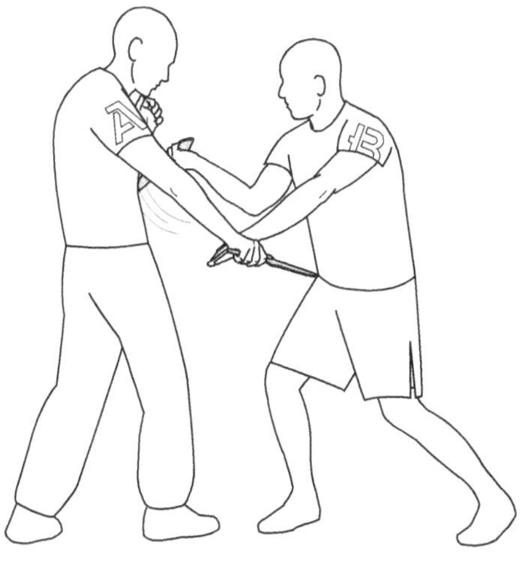

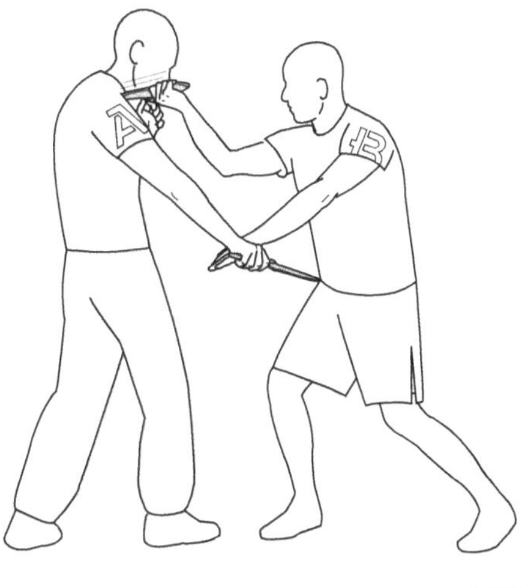

A serves an angle 5 stab to the abdomen
B deflects the attack with his unarmed hand while getting out of the line of attack by the outside, or with his unarmed forearm by the inside
B does simultaneously a slash to the arm of A between his hand and the shoulder of A
B doubles his slash to the arm and follows with a stab to the body

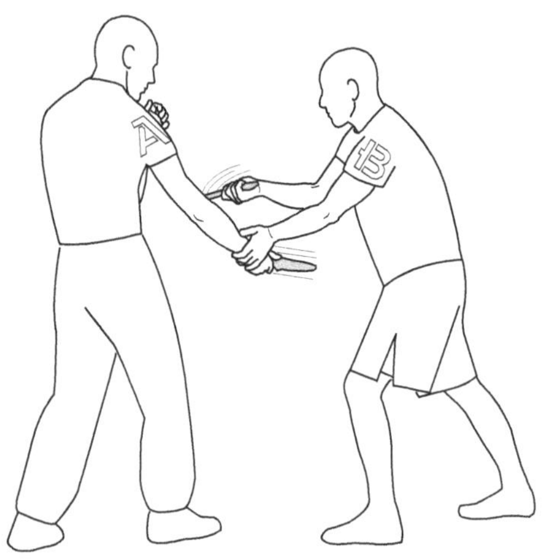

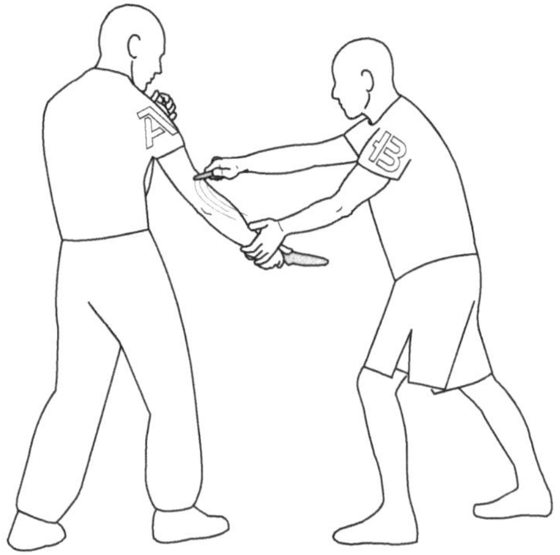

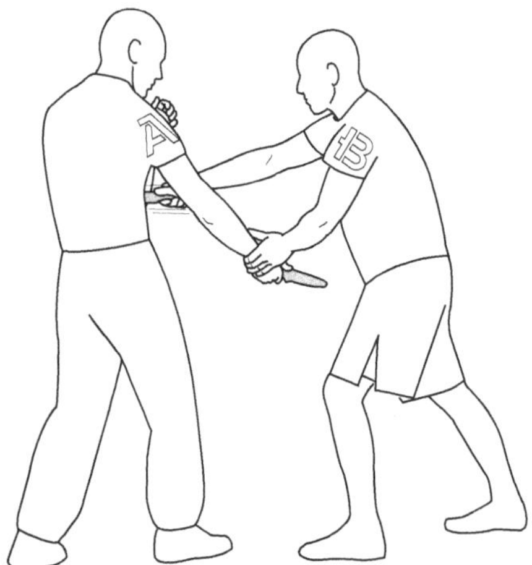

A and B exchange their roles

VARIATION

A holds his weapon in Hammer grip, but B takes his knife in Ice Pick grip

COMBATIVE EXERCISE

In the previous exercise, the blocks were done with the unarmed forearm. In this one, we block with the arm on the side where the attack comes, as in the natural block.

Furthermore, instead of doing counterattacks with slashes in the forearm, not necessarily relevant facing an opponent wearing thick clothes, we will immediately stab.

A and B are armed with a knife and hold it in Hammer grip.

Medio Contrada range
A serves an angle 1 slash to the throat
B blocks with his unarmed forearm, while purchasing some distance, and simultaneously stabs in the hollow of the shoulder
B redirects the armed arm of A with his armed hand from below, then controls the arm at the elbow with his Check of his empty hand (getting so his blade free)
B serves two stabs in the side

A serves an angle 4 slash to the abdomen
B blocks with his armed arm, while purchasing some distance
B checks at the elbow with his empty hand to free his blade
B serves two stabs to the liver
B serves a stab to the throat

We take care not to lose contact with the armed arm of the opponent to protect ourselves of an attempt of riposte. If the armed hand does the block, the Check with the empty hand comes to free it and keeps the control during the stabs.

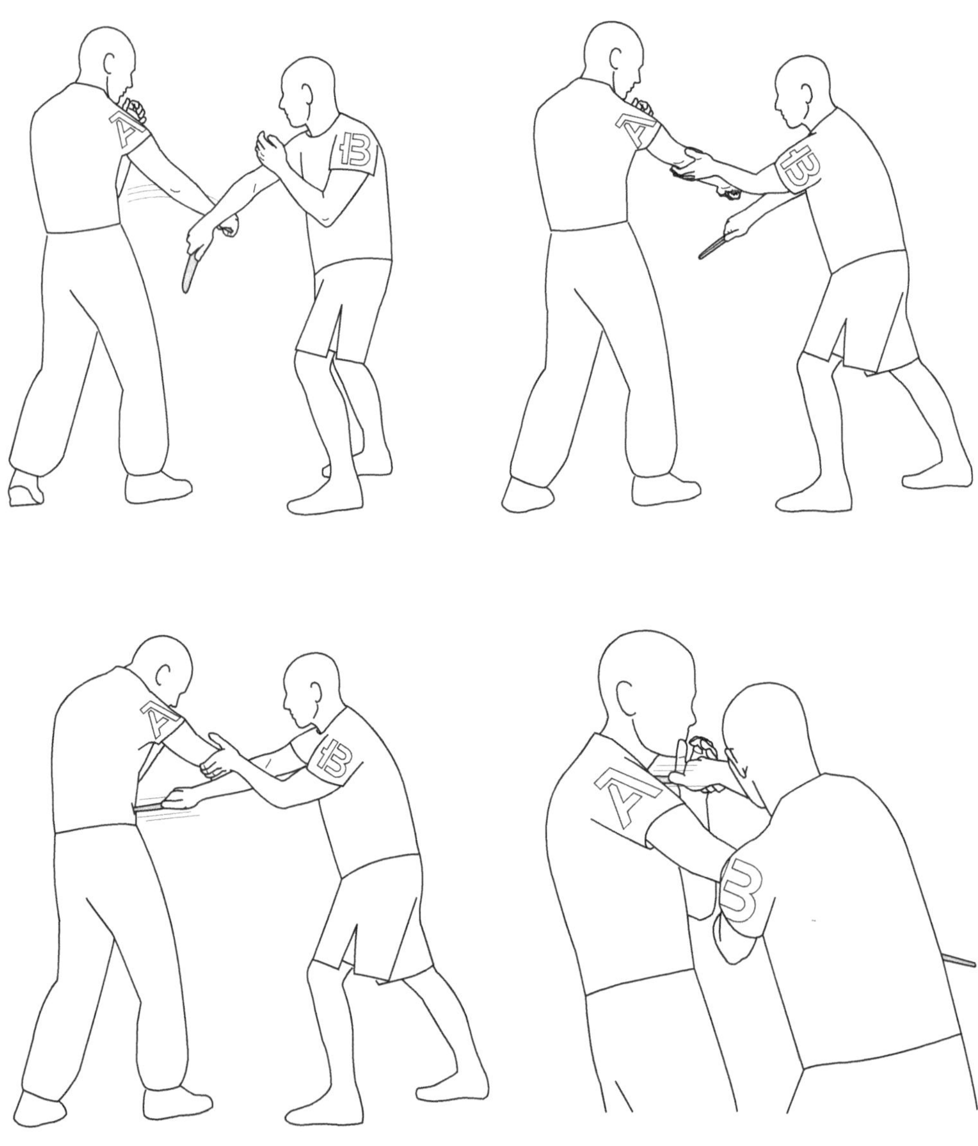

A serves an angle 3 slash to the abdomen
B blocks with his unarmed forearm, while purchasing some distance, and stabs in the hollow of the shoulder
B redirects the armed arm of A with his armed hand from above, then controls the arm at the elbow with a Check of his empty hand
B serves two stabs in the side

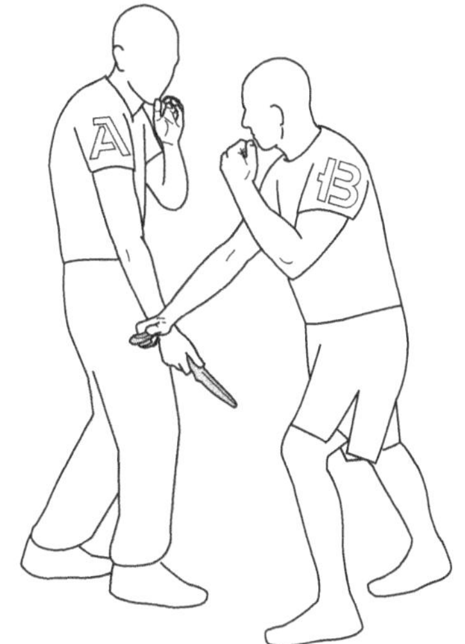
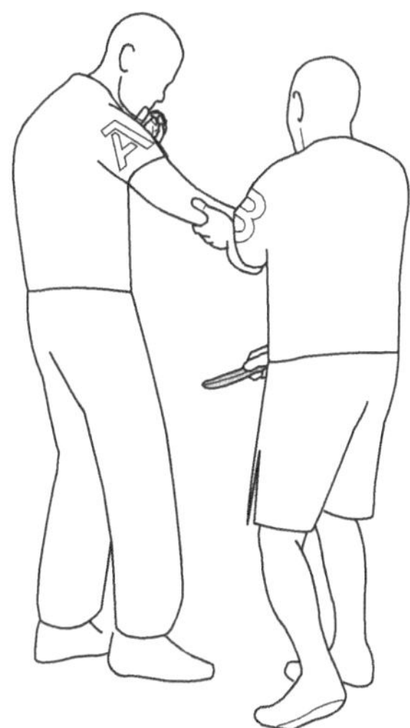

A serves an angle 2 slash to the throat
B blocks with his armed forearm, while purchasing some distance
B checks at the elbow with his empty hand,
getting his armed hand free
B moves down the arm of A and stabs two
times to the throat

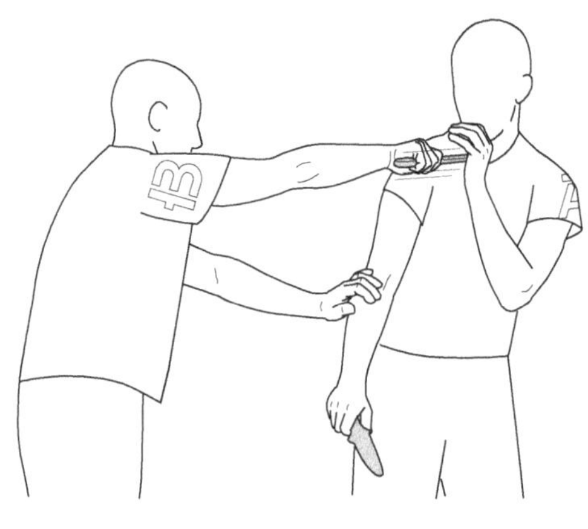

A serves an angle 5 stab to the abdomen
B gets out of the line of attack by the outside while deflecting the blade with a
Check at the elbow of A, and stabs two times to the abdomen

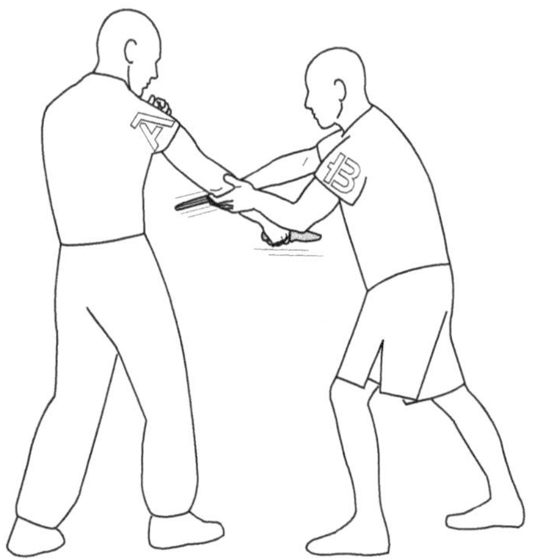

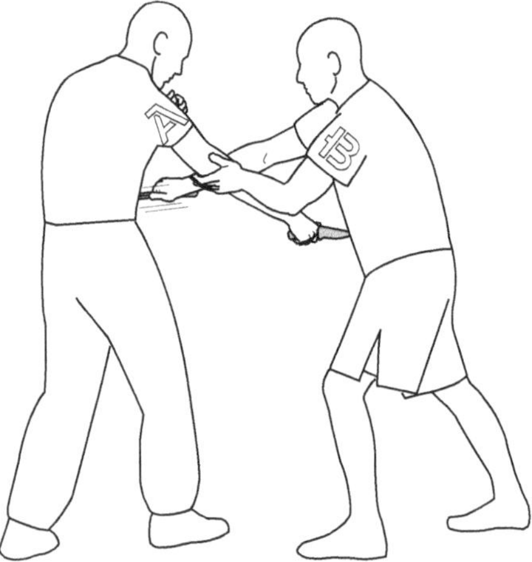

III. DRILLS

SUMBRADA 5

It is a 'your turn / my turn' exercise on 5 attacks. For the good execution of the drill, we deliberately place ourselves in a biased range, that is clearly not a range of engagement in a knife fight. We must differentiate between the exercise, the drill, and the fight (if it needs to be repeated).

A and B are armed with a knife held in the right hand in Hammer grip.

Medio Contrada range
A serves an angle 1 slash
B counters in Crossada with a slash
B serves an angle 1 slash
A counters in Palis with a slash
A serves an angle 4 slash
B counters with an opening Crossada with a slash
B serves an angle 5 stab
A counters with a closing Crossada with a slash
A serves an angle 2 stab
B counters with a Check that pushes the wrist of A on his blade
B serves an angle 1 slash
A counters in Crossada…

Sumbrada 5

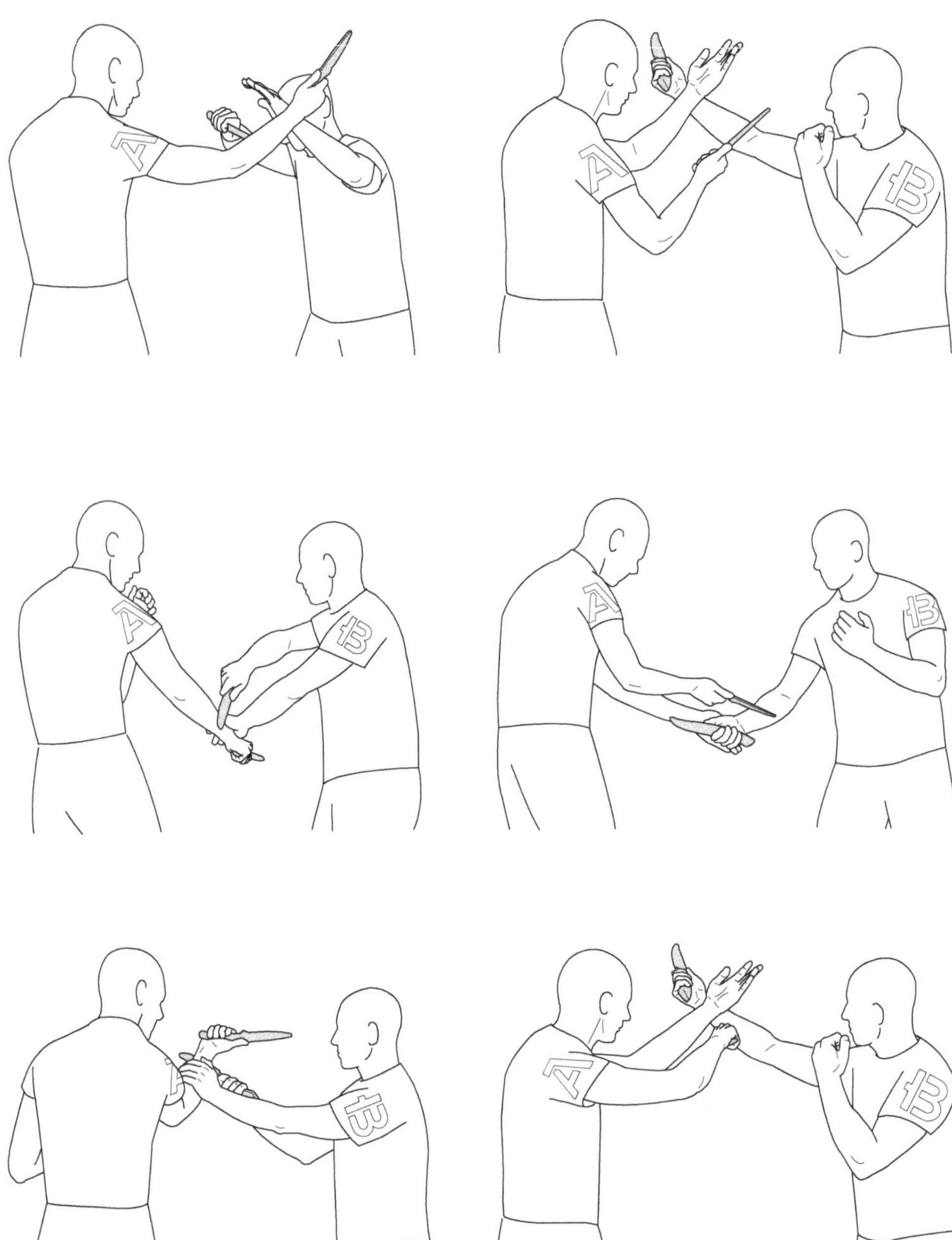

CUT & SLASH

We are here on an intermediate level drill that starts to be close to sparring, but still is not. It is a dynamic training, free, but still codified. For example, we try hard to do readable attacks for the partner to train well.

A and B are armed with a knife and train with slashing attacks, choosing freely the angle, on a 'your turn / my turn' principle. The attack is done to the throat, to the body or to the leg. The counterattack is done to the arm. The important thing is not to be hit by the attack. The counterattack is secondary.

Range of engagement Largo Mano
A serves a slash
B protects himself (block or parry) and slashes the armed arm of A simultaneously
B serves a slash
A protects himself and slashes the armed arm of B simultaneously
A serves a slash, B protects himself…

Drills

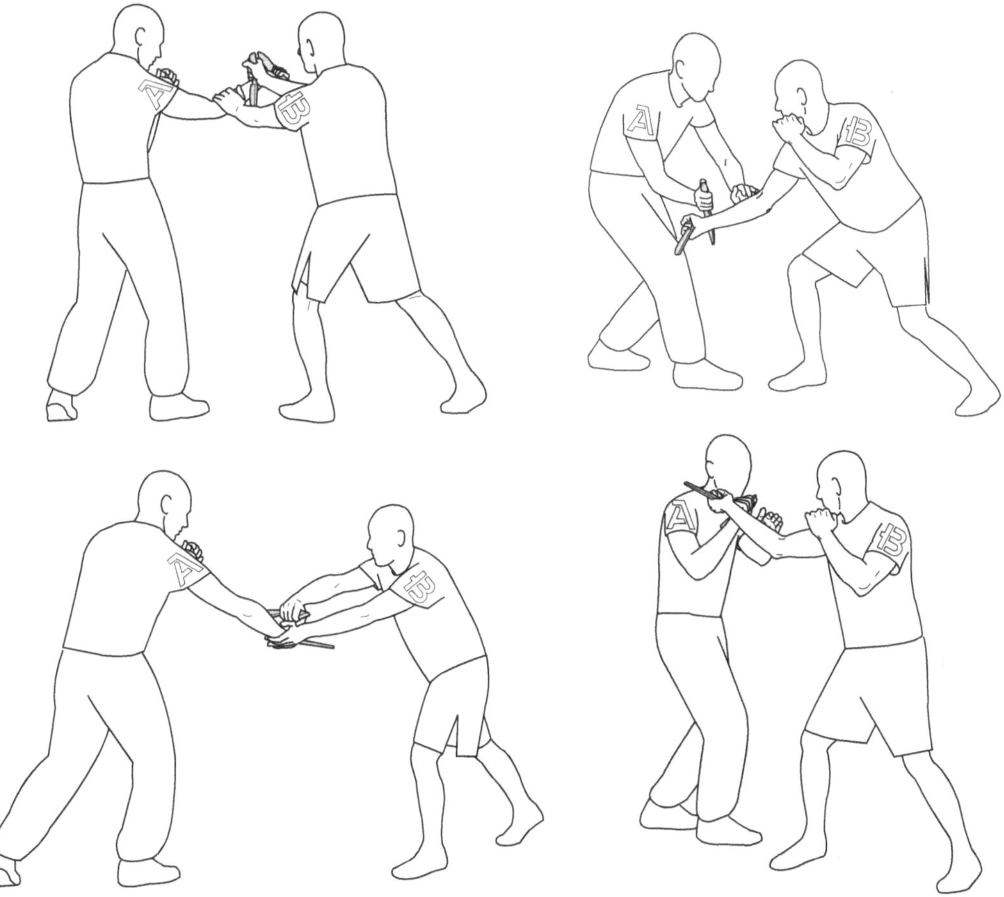

STAB & SLASH

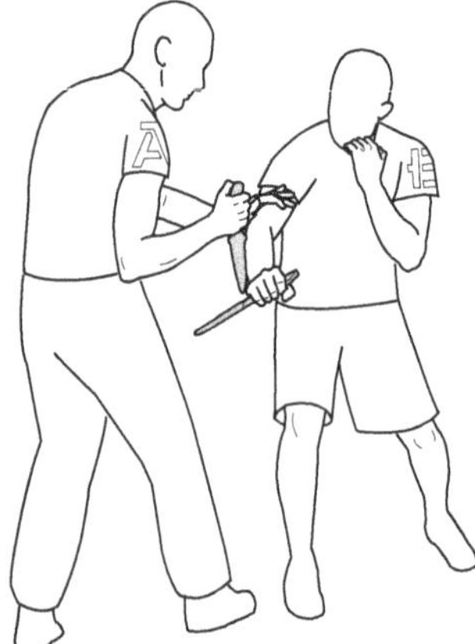

Same exercise as for Cut & Slash, but the two partners use only stabs in their attacks.

Range of engagement Largo Mano
B serves a stab
A protects himself (block or parry) and cuts the armed arm of B simultaneously
A serves a stab
B protects himself and slashes the armed arm of A simultaneously
…

CUT OR STAB & SLASH

We mix the two previous drills to let the expression of the two partners be more and more free.

Range of engagement Largo Mano
B serves a slash or a stab
A protects himself (block or parry) and slashes the armed arm of B simultaneously
A serves a slash or a stab
B protects himself and slashes the armed arm of A simultaneously
…

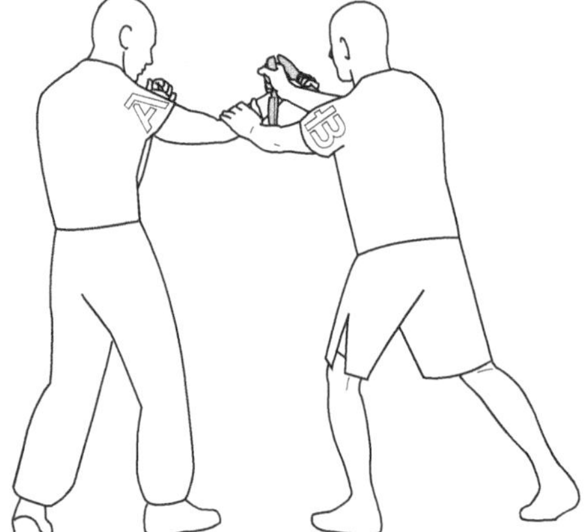

IV. Applications

Against Angle 1 attack

A are B armed with a knife.

Largo Mano range
A (Hammer grip) serves an angle 1 stab to the throat
B (Ice Pick grip) blocks with his unarmed forearm, while purchasing some distance, and counterattacks with a slash to the tendon above the elbow
B redirects the arm of A with the back of his blade, then with a Check at the elbow (getting so his weapon free)
B serves a slash to the throat
B picks up the hand of A with the back of his blade and seizes the fleshy part of the thumb of A with his empty hand
B causes the disarm with a slash to the tendons of the wrist

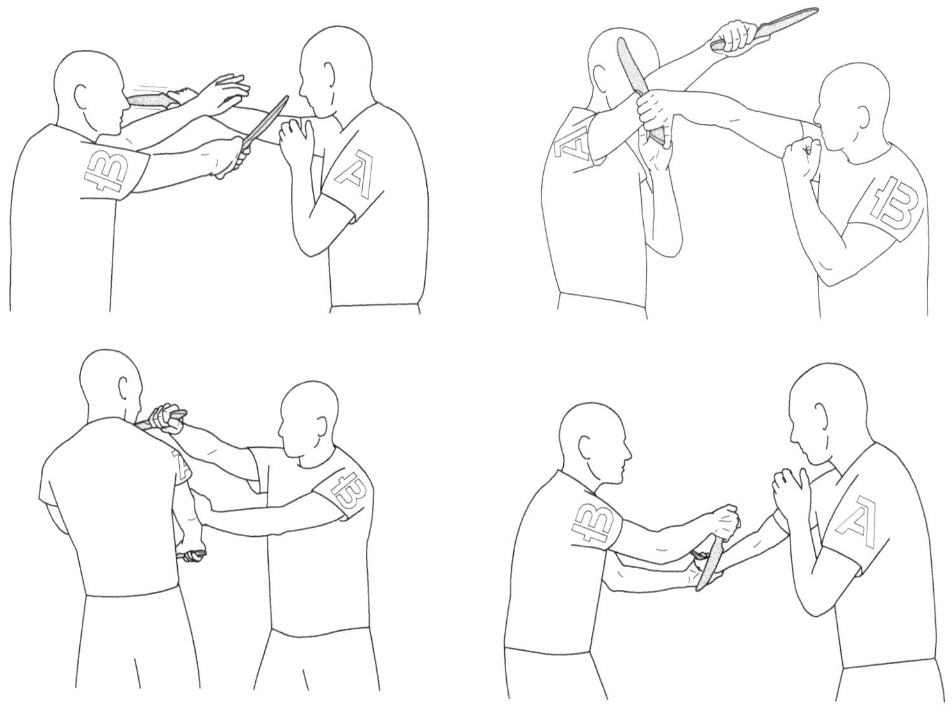

AGAINST ANGLE 3 ATTACK

Largo Mano range
A (Hammer grip) serves an angle 3 stab to the abdomen
B (Ice Pick grip) blocks with his unarmed forearm, while purchasing some distance, and counterattacks with an ascending slash to the tendon above the elbow
B picks up the forearm of A with the back of his blade and redirects the arm towards the body, as if he was serving a stab to the thigh of A. He changes his control on the arm for a pressure with his unarmed forearm (getting his weapon free)
B serves a slash to the throat
B picks up the wrist of A with his armed hand, using a 'lighter' grip, to bring it to his empty hand.
B serves a slash to the thigh
B causes the disarm with a slash to the tendons of the armed wrist of A

During the manipulation, seizure, control and redirection, of the armed arm of A, there is always the idea that we can interchange our hands to maintain the contact. A pick up with the back of the blade is followed by a Check. A redirection with the armed hand brings to the empty hand... The idea being to control, and so to protect ourselves from the blade of the opponent, without letting it free, and to bring it where we want to cause the disarm. Here, for that matter we use a slash immediately incapacitating of the tendons, because we are armed, instead of trying a complicated disarm.

The seizure of the armed hand of A with the empty hand is done at the fleshy part of the thumb and not at the wrist. So, the mobility of the hand and of the blade is limited, and most importantly we don't cut ourselves during the disarm.

Disarm the opponent, 'defanging the snake' to quote the expression of the Filipino eskrimadors, or cancel his ability to use his weapon against us is incidentally one of the priority goals. A blade, and notably a short one, remains dangerous without inertia, and can easily be used even by an opponent who comes off worst. So, even in an application that is quite technical — allowing the eskrimador to train his dexterity and his array of counterattacks — we favor the slashes to the arm and to the armed wrist.

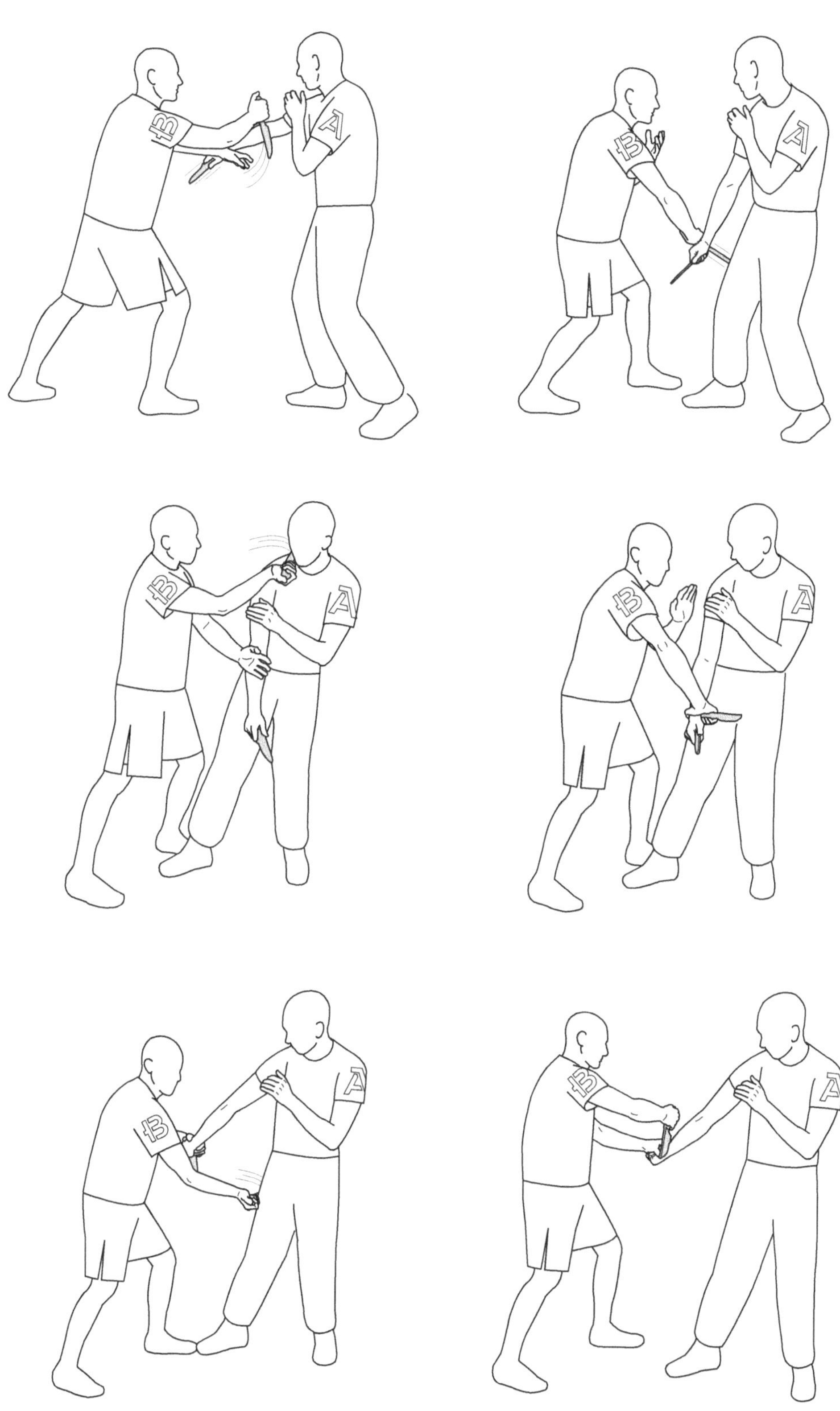

Against Angle 4 attack

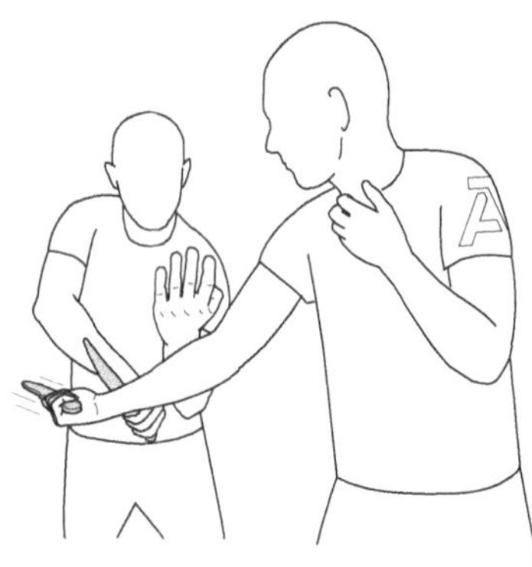

Largo Mano range

A (Hammer grip) serves an angle 4 stab to the abdomen

B (Ice Pick grip) blocks with his unarmed forearm, while purchasing some distance, and counterattacks with a descending slash to the armed forearm of A

B comes back with an ascending slash to the forearm of A

B picks up the wrist of A with the back of his blade and redirects the arm, then checks with a pressure towards the body of A, blocking the arm and freeing his own blade

B serves a slash to the throat

B picks up the armed hand of A with a 'lighter grip', then causes the disarm with a slash to the tendons of the wrist

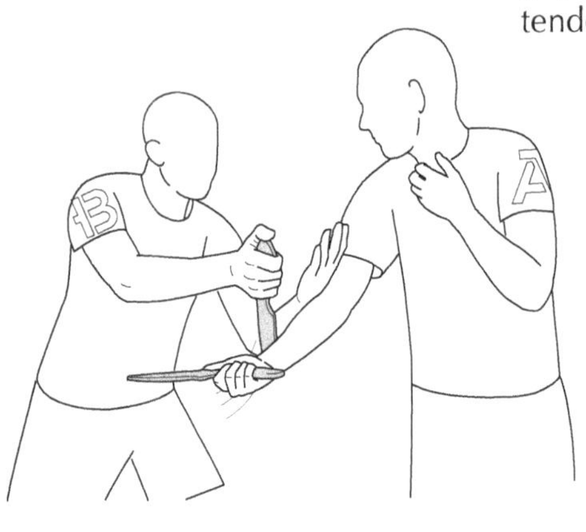

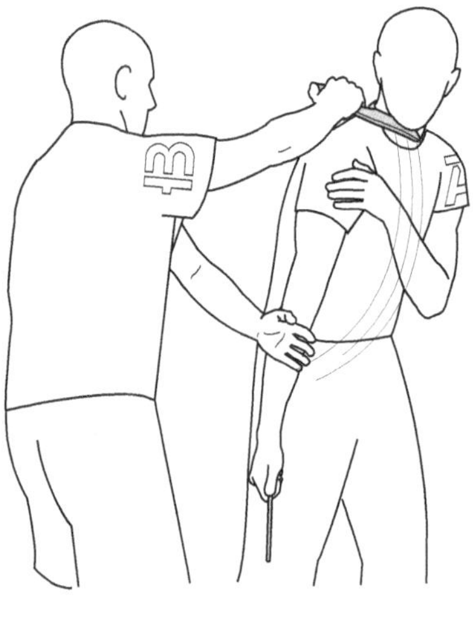

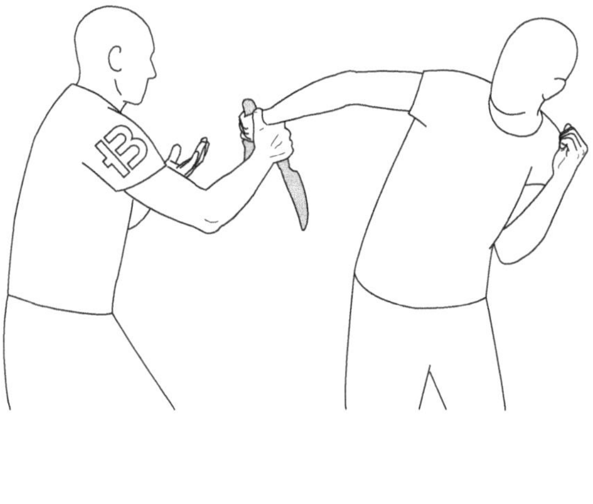

Against Angle 2 attack

Largo Mano range

A (Hammer grip) serves an angle 2 stab to the throat

B (Ice Pick grip) blocks with his unarmed forearm, while purchasing some distance, and counterattacks with an ascending slash to the forearm of A

B picks up the forearm of A with the back of his blade and redirects the arm towards the body as if he was serving a stab to the thigh of A. He changes his control on the arm for a pressure with his unarmed forearm (getting his weapon free)

B serves a slash to the throat

B picks up the wrist of A with his armed hand to bring it to his empty hand

B causes the disarm with a slash to the tendons of the armed wrist of A

Applications

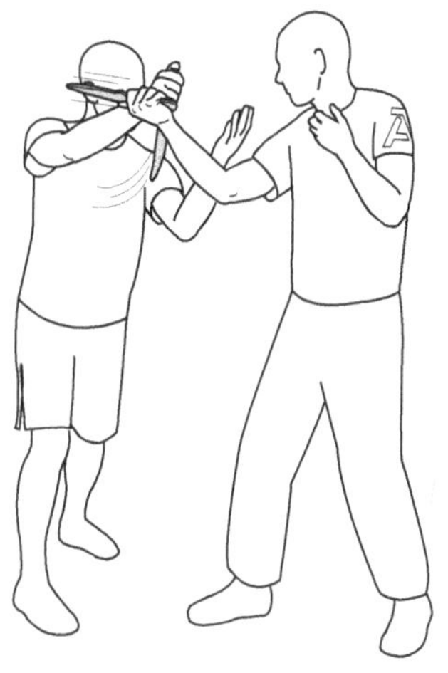

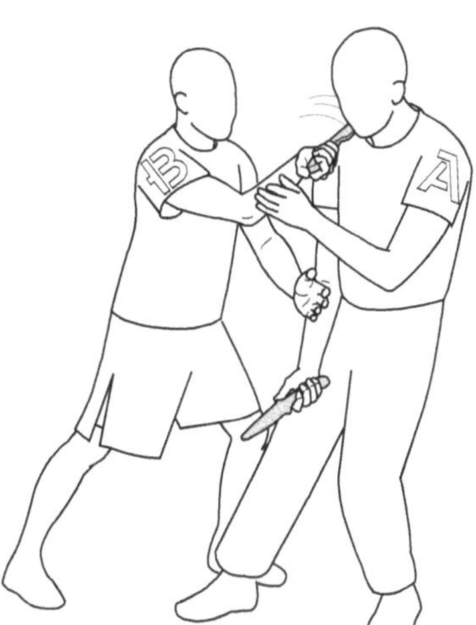
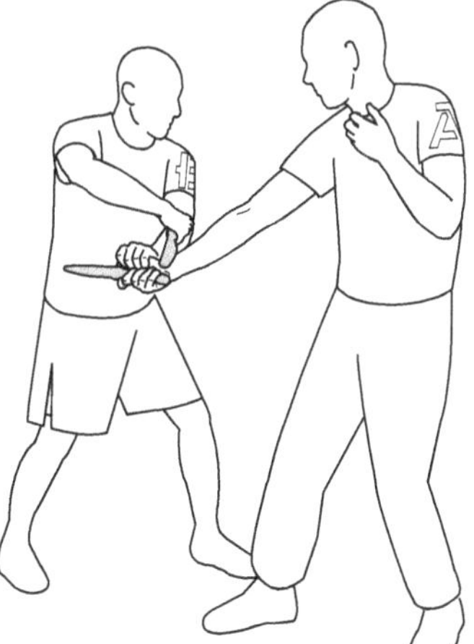

Against Angle 5 attack

Largo Mano range
A (Hammer grip) attacks with an angle 5 stab to the abdomen
B counters with his unarmed hand inside or outside the guard of A, while purchasing some distance
B serves a slash to the forearm of A
…

Sparring

If we have favored training aluminum knives in the previous exercises for the realistic contact of cold metal. That same contact can quickly become unpleasant during a sparring at full speed. So, for that kind of exchange we choose to use knives with a wooden core wrapped in thick foam, like the Nok model. We also use protective eyewear.

Finally, for the exercise to be useful, each of the participant must take it up being aware that the weapon used are far (quite fortunately) from causing the damages of a live blade — and train consequently when hit, and according to the area reached. Change the hand that holds the weapon when 'injured' to the armed arm is relevant… serve multiple stabs to the opponent when we have been indisputably touched at the throat… much less.

As we have seen, we first take care of our protection by stepping out and keeping the targets away, waiting for an opportunity to riposte and hit an incapacitating or lethal area.

The one that is the less injured… wins…

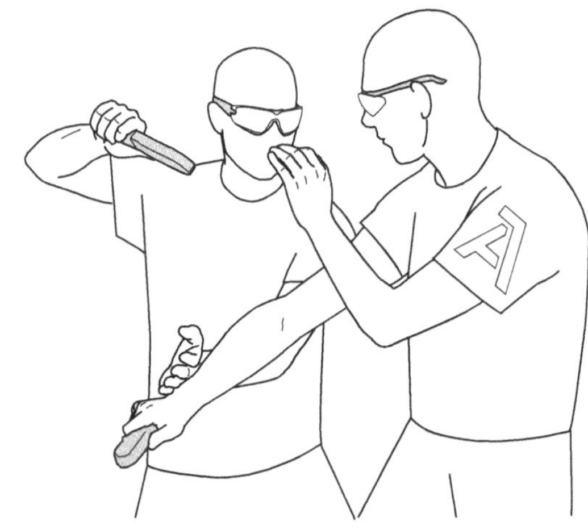

Mano-Mano, Espada y Daga...
Stick Fighting

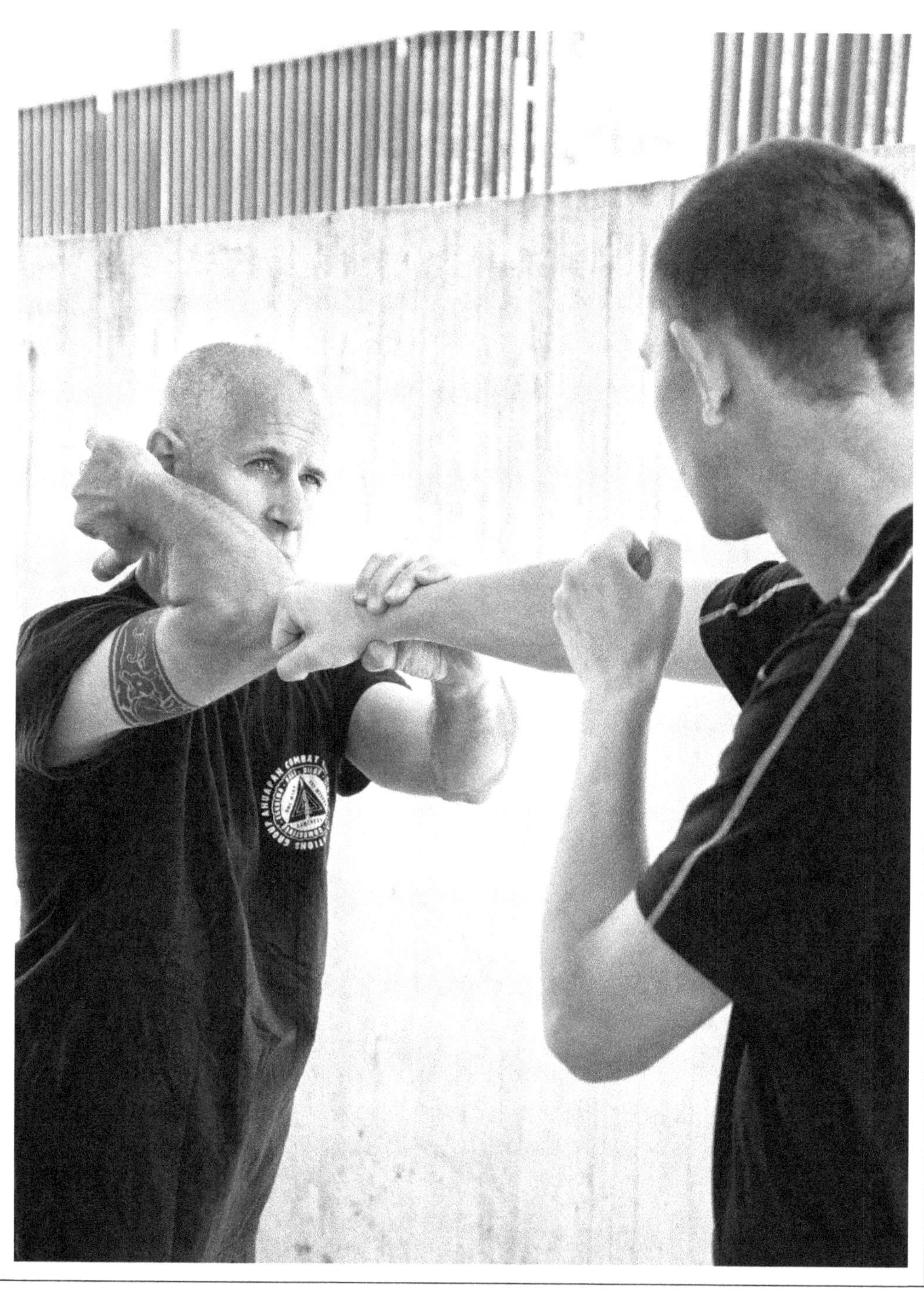

BY WAY OF CONCLUSION

A confrontation knife against knife is not a normal configuration. In the setting of an aggression with a knife, the engagement will almost always be an attacker armed with a knife against a person bare hands, even if only the time to apply a weapon of his own (newspaper, belt, bag, a piece of wood…). Yet, in a bare hands against knife configuration, the body mechanics trained all through the previous chapter will be the same, although the damages caused by the ripostes will be lesser.

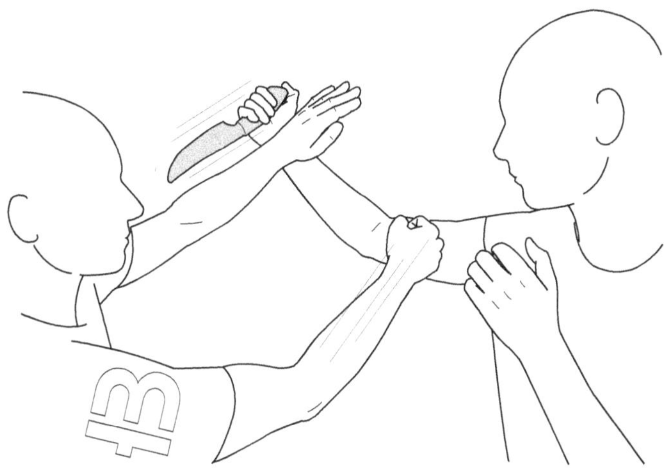

We hope this book to be a sound introduction to the work of the Ahuapan Combat Eskrima group and Filipino Martial Arts in general. But it cannot cover the whole of the wealth of techniques developed and taught. In the logic of the FMA, it represents the acquisition of the basics while offering an almost endless training material.

The training of Solo Baston allows to become aware of combat ranges, to acquire correct angles of strike, to start to move while taking account of the presence of a weapon, in our own hand, as in the one of the opponent. The Doble Baston complete that with the coordination of the two upper limbs, the ambidexterity and a new perspective of the management of the space. The empty hand had started to come to life with the Check in Solo Baston, it now works entirely while holding a weapon. And it becomes essential facing a Knife, being both a target to be protected from the blade of the opponent and an asset to control and redirect his armed arm to allow opportunities of riposte.

All these skills are acquired for the work of bare hands against bare hands of the FMA, Mano-Mano, that result from the training with the weapons. They also constitute the basics to take on the bare hands against weapons exchanges, the training with two weapons of different length like the sword and the dagger, Espada y Daga, or else the handling of the staff, the Sibat…

These practices enrich the technical array of the eskrimador and his perception of the different situations that he may encounter. They also enhance his understanding and his mastery of the combat ranges, the footworks, his coordination and his body mechanics. And, by a fair reward, they so allow to strengthen our basics and our ease with Solo Baston, Doble Baston and Knife, while bringing more diversity to the trainings and keeping the mind stimulated.

In order to highlight the national martial arts, the Filipino government has, in the middle of the 20th century, encouraged the development of their competitive form. The friendly exchanges, or quite less friendly, between masters or eskrimadors of two villages moved so to stadiums and gymnasiums. Rules, classes and specific protections were established. Nowadays, Not only a World Championship, organized by the World Eskrima Kali Arnis Federation, exists but also continental competitions, like the European Championship, or national, as the French Cup under the aegis of the 'Fédération Française de Karaté'.

In 2002, Thomas Roussel won the World Championship title, in addition to his three European Championship titles. His understanding of martial arts and his mastery of Stick Fighting serve now the Ahuapan Combat Eskrima group that counts several competitors holding titles in recent European an World competitions.

Glossary

There is spelling variations for some terms, but also definition variations between one school and another. This glossary is established to detail the Filipino or English terms as they are used in this book, and among the Ahuapan Combat Eskrima group.

Abaniko : snapped strike with a quick rotation of the wrist.

Abecedario : the basics.

Abierta : the open guard.

Arko : rotation move of the wrist in the strike.

Arnis : term referring to the FMA, see also Eskrima and Kali.

Carenza : shadow boxing of the eskrima.

Check : to check / make contact with our unarmed hand.

Corto : short range.

Doble Baston : double sticks.

Drill : educational exercise / sequence with a partner.

Eskrima : term referring to the FMA, see also Arnis and Kali.

Eskrimador : who trains in eskrima.

Espada y Daga : sword and dagger, training with a long weapon and a short weapon.

Guro : instructor.

Kali : term referring to the FMA, see also Arnis and Eskrima.

Kurbada : circular strike.

Lobtik : going through strike.

Largo Mano : long range.

Medio Contrada : medium range.

Numerado : numbering system of the angles.

Olisi : stick.

Panantukan : Filipino boxing.

Punong Guro : head instructor.

Punyo : the butt of the stick.

Redondo : circular strike on the vertical axis, backhand.

Retirada Caballero : glided footwork, the half-step.

Retirada Ilustrisimo : walked footwork, the step.

Serrada : the closed guard.

Sibat : staff.

Sinawali : Doble Baston.

Solo Baston : single stick.

Witik : snapped strike.

By joint agreement, the authors of this book have decided to renounce a part of their royalties in favor of the Filipino archipelago and its population.

Hagane is so entrusted with the task to reserve that part and use the raised funds to take on a share of the financing of humanitarian aids, and cultural or sporting actions, depending on the news and the needs.

THANKS

A very big thank-you to Romain Frola, for his availability during the whole creation of this book.

A big thank-you too to the correctors team, Léa, Anthony, Christian and Morgana for their sharped eyes, their advices and their support — not forgetting Robert for his help on the English version.